ROOTED
— *IN* —
HOPE

A

PUBLICATION

Editorial Director: Elizabeth Foss

Designed by: Kristin Foss and Carly Buckholz

Copy Editors: Katy Greiner, Stephen Foss and Nick Foss

Illustration, Cover art & Calligraphy: Carolyn Svellinger

Research & Development: Katherine Johnson

ISBN-13:978-1975746742

ISBN-10:1975746740

take up & READ
C O M M U N I T Y

VISIT US
takeupandread.org

BE SOCIAL
Facebook @takeupandread

Instagram @takeupandread

Twitter @totakeupandread

SEND A NOTE
totakeupandread@gmail.com

CONNECT
#TakeUpAndRead

#RootedinHope

GATHER A GROUP
Group Guides will be available at takeupandread.org as our gift to you.

ROOTED IN HOPE FOR KIDS
For your children, we will have printable children's books

available for free at takeupandread.org

WELCOME TO OUR NEW DESIGN

In this scripture study, we wanted to connect you deeply with the Word and help you plan to stay connected throughout the busy Advent season. We added brand ndew design layouts and planner pages to ensure you have the tools to keep Him close to your heart everyday.

ROOTS & BRANCHES

This page roots the study in tradition, providing background as you begin.

SCRIPTURE READING

This scripture study includes daily Scripture readings, ready with margins and extra space for all of your notes and commentary. Notations for further reading are provided so you can dig deeper.

LECTIO DIVINA

Reflect upon the Word and make a deep connection with your daily life.

ACTIO

Make a plan to take action, allowing God to seep into every part of your day.

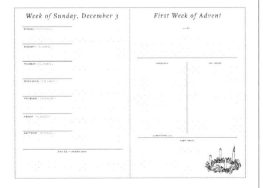

WEEKLY PLANNER

We created space for you to write out the week's memory verse, a list of prayer requests, and space for your plans to give + prepare.

Inhale! Here on the doorstep of December, inhale the crispness of the season. Bright with hope, we promise ourselves: this year will be different. This year, we'll remember the Advent candles, and they'll be on the wreath and ready on the first Sunday. This year, we'll finish shopping and wrapping well before the guests come so that we're not squirreled away in our room at the eleventh hour wondering whatever happened to to the tape and why we ran out of ribbon. But mostly, this year, we'll arrive at the creche on Christmas Eve peaceful and recollected. The meaning of the Savior will be sunk so deeply into our hearts that we will overflow with the genuine joy.

At Take Up & Read, we're hoping all those things, too. And we created this unique prayer journal and planner with those hopes in mind. In your hands, you hold the tool to integrate all the busy details of the season with all the prayerful intentions of an Advent rooted in hope. Seamlessly integrated into tools of prayer are the practical tools of planning for action. This journal acknowledges that you are a busy woman who has much to do.

And it asks you to press "pause," to pray, and then to plan to do exactly what God intends each day. We'll step you through the age-old, time-tested method of prayer called "lectio divina" and then we'll take you from contemplation to active participation in seamless movements.

But before we settle in to see the details of this prayer plan, I want to acknowledge that there will be days when you don't "fill in all the blanks." Throughout this book, we have placed tools for bringing lectio divina to life in your life--right now in the busiest of seasons. Intentionally, we gave you more to do, even though we know you are very busy. That's the paradox of prayer: when you take the time to pray, God shows you where you have time to do what it is important. Please take this a day at a time, even a moment at a time. Maybe you will focus on one part of the Lectio Divina in the morning and leave all the other spaces blank. And then, maybe, you will find a small pocket of time in the afternoon to engage once again, discovering that you've carried the Word with you all day, and it is bearing fruit, and those fruitful thoughts spill onto your pages. This is your book. Pray your way.

Little by little, let the examples of the holy prophets whose stories are told in this book inspire you. They didn't travel a straight and perfect path. They stumbled, and they fell. But God used each and every one of them in the great arc of the salvation story. He's using you, too. Every day, with every decision.

Pray. Then be open to His plan, and see how it can become your plan.

December Two

sunday	monday	tuesday
26	27	28
3 FIRST SUNDAY OF ADVENT	4	5
10 SECOND SUNDAY OF ADVENT	11	12 OUR LADY OF GUADALUPE
17 THIRD SUNDAY OF ADVENT	18	19
24 FOURTH SUNDAY OF ADVENT CHRISTMAS EVE	25 **NATIVITY OF THE LORD** CHRISTMAS DAY	26 FEAST OF SAINT STEPHEN
31 FEAST OF THE HOLY FAMILY NEW YEAR'S EVE	1	2

Thousand Seventeen

wednesday	thursday	friday	saturday
29	30	1	2
6 FEAST OF SAINT NICHOLAS	7 FEAST OF SAINT AMBROSE	8 **HOLY DAY OF OBLIGATION** THE IMMACULATE CONCEPTION OF THE BLESSED VIRGIN MARY	9 FEAST OF SAINT JUAN DIEGO
13 FEAST OF SAINT LUCY	14 FEAST OF SAINT JOHN OF THE CROSS	15	16
20	21	22	23 FEAST OF SAINT JOHN OF KANTY
27 FEAST OF SAINT JOHN	28 FEAST OF THE HOLY INNOCENTS	29	30
3	4	5	6

Thursday, November 30
ROOTS & BRANCHES

St. Andrew Novena

Hail, and blessed be the hour and moment
at which the Son of God was born
of a most pure Virgin Mary at a stable at midnight
in Bethlehem in the piercing cold.
At that hour vouchsafe, I beseech Thee,
to hear my prayers and grant my desires.

(*Mention your intentions here*)

Through Jesus Christ and
His most Blessed Mother.
Amen.

LUKE 2:4-7

Joseph also went from the town of Nazareth in Galilee to Judea, to the city of David called Bethlehem, because he was descended from the house and family of David. He went to be registered with Mary, to whom he was engaged and who was expecting a child. While they were there, the time came for her to deliver her child. And she gave birth to her firstborn son and wrapped him in bands of cloth, and laid him in a manger, because there was no place for them in the inn.

PSALM 46:10

"Be still, and know that I am God! I am exalted among the nations, I am exalted in the earth.

FOR FURTHER READING

LUKE 1:4-7

With this study, we begin before the beginning because Advent is still a few days away. This year, the shortened season means that the traditional date for beginning the Saint Andrew Christmas prayer falls outside the Advent season. We use these grace days to set the scene.

Traditionally, this contemplative prayer is to be prayed fifteen times a day, every day during Advent. It is neither magical nor superstitious. Nothing terrible will befall you or your family if "you break the chain." But something miraculous might happen if you develop the habit of contemplating the manger over the next 25 days.

When you say this prayer, put yourself inside of it. Be there in that holy hour and moment. Look around you. Smell the smells. Sit inside the stable warmed by the steam of an animal's nostrils. Feel the exquisite softness of infant skin. Kiss the top of his perfect downy head.

Feel, too, the piercing cold—the hardened hearts of those who shut this holy threesome out at the time of need. Know the burdens they bore to get to this place. Know the burdens that lie ahead of them.

With this passage of Scripture, begin to cultivate in your heart a habit of lectio divina, the art of reading the divine Scripture with the intention of knowing what it really says, knowing what God wants you, uniquely to hear, knowing what to say to Him in response, and knowing what to do about it all. With this beginning, resolve this Advent to know, in the truest sense of the word.

Your life, no doubt, is about to be very busy. In this small space between the Thanksgiving holiday weekend and the First Sunday of Advent, there is already a palpable quickening to the beat of our days. You are making lists and jotting notes, capturing ideas on paper or on Pinterest. You are likely shopping—hopefully you have remembered to put Advent candles on your late-November list. They will almost certainly be unavailable next week. On one of those lists, make a plan to be still.

Plan to sit with Scripture and let it seep into your being.

Plan to quiet your racing mind and your busy hands and feet and just be.

Plan to revisit this plan every day.

In order to enter fully into the miracle of Christmas, endeavor to enter fully into Scripture during Advent. Let yourself steep in the Word. Take your time. Light a candle, fix a drink of something hot and hold it in your hands (a timeless trick for staying awake). Read your Bible with the fullest attention you can summon, carefully noting the author's intent and the literary value each book holds. Meditate upon it with a clear, active mind, searching it for the truth God has hidden there. Let the Word move your heart toward prayer in a way that unites it with God and makes Him a part of you, and you more and more like Him. Ask Him into your interior spaces and let Him clear away the debris He finds there and replace it with His holy wholeness. Contemplate the Word with a mind that lifts above the scurrying of your busy whirlwind and rests serenely in the peace of Christ.

These are lofty goals, to be sure, lofty aspirations for a season where so much is already dictated to us by the duties of our vocations. But they are essential goals. They are the pegs upon which a peaceful Advent hangs. They are the very disciplines the Lord desires so that He can reveal Himself to you.

ELIZABETH FOSS

CULTIVATE

How will I cultivate a daily habit of lectio divina?

When can I plan to make time for the Word, God and myself each day?

What is my motivation to continute my scripture study practice?

PREPARE

How will I prepare for the piercing cold?

When do I struggle the most during Advent?

How can I bring grace and love to the hard days?

SAVOR

How will I slow down and savor?

How can I remind myself to savor the season?

What brings me peace when Advent feels hectic?

GROW

How will I grow closer to Christ this Advent?

Where will I find quiet moments, alone with God?

How do I see Christ's fingerprints in my daily life?

I will forgive myself for

I will forgive others for

COMMIT + PLAN

I am grateful for

---

this Advent, I am saying "yes" to

this Advent, I am saying "no" to

I will let go of perfection in these ways

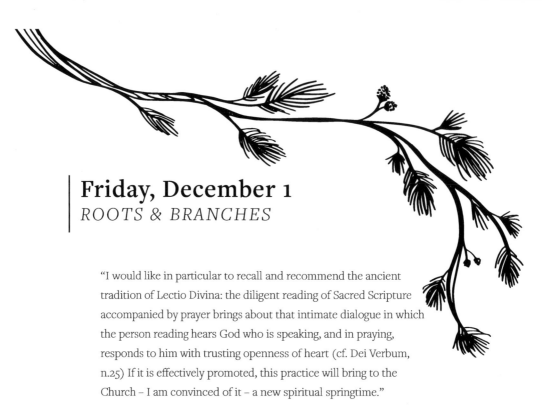

Friday, December 1
ROOTS & BRANCHES

"I would like in particular to recall and recommend the ancient tradition of Lectio Divina: the diligent reading of Sacred Scripture accompanied by prayer brings about that intimate dialogue in which the person reading hears God who is speaking, and in praying, responds to him with trusting openness of heart (cf. Dei Verbum, n.25) If it is effectively promoted, this practice will bring to the Church – I am convinced of it – a new spiritual springtime."

Pope Benedict XVI

Devote yourself to the lectio of the divine Scriptures; apply yourself to this with perseverance. Do your reading with the intent of believing in and pleasing God. If during the lectio you encounter a closed door, knock and it will be opened to you by that guardian of whom Jesus said, 'The gatekeeper will open it for him'. By applying yourself in this way to lectio divina, search diligently and with unshakable trust in God for the meaning of the divine Scriptures, which is hidden in great fullness within. You ought not, however, to be satisfied merely with knocking and seeking: to understand the things of God, what is absolutely necessary is oratio. For this reason, the Saviour told us not only: 'Seek and you will find', and 'Knock and it shall be opened to you', but also added, 'Ask and you shall receive'"

Origen of Alexandria

DEUTERONOMY 30:14

No, the word is very near to you; it is in your mouth and in your heart for you to observe.

2 TIMOTHY 3:14-16

But as for you, continue in what you have learned and firmly believed, knowing from whom you learned it, and how from childhood you have known the sacred writings that are able to instruct you for salvation through faith in Christ Jesus. All scripture is inspired by God and is useful for teaching, for reproof, for correction, and for training in righteousness, so that everyone who belongs to God may be proficient, equipped for every good work.

ROMANS 15:4

For whatever was written in former days was written for our instruction, so that by steadfastness and by the encouragement of the scriptures we might have hope.

FOR FURTHER READING:

1 CORINTHIANS 2:9

PSALMS 36:7-9

Together, as a community of faithful women, today in the first week of December, we are ready for a spiritual springtime. We are ready for new life—for a spiritual renewal of our minds, hearts, and souls. We are embracing Advent in the truest meaning of the word: this will be the time for an arrival of a notable person, and He will take up residence in our very beings and fill us to overflowing with Himself.

How? How will the tired soul living in the woman who has come to the end of the secular year be energized by the beginning of the liturgical year? How will she do it while staring down the million and one things women have to do this time of year?

She will pray—more. That's right. She will take more time to pray at the very time of year when time seems so short. Can we do that together? Can we take up for ourselves the ancient tradition of lectio divina and let the Word lead us to live in charity? We can and we must. This is the best way to prepare ourselves to greet the Babe with peaceful composure and serene grace.

In his 2010 apostolic exhortation Verbum Domini, Pope Benedict VXI beautifully instructs the faithful to prayerfully read the Scripture. Following his lead, we will be drawn into a practice that is as old as Scripture itself.

In the early Christian communities, Scripture was read to nourish faith with the wisdom of truth. When we hold the New Testament, we take up the understanding that the first Christians had of the Old Testament, together with the divine revelation the Holy Spirit granted to Jesus' earliest followers.

The Church Fathers' faith was informed by their careful, prayerful reading of the Word. Today, we are blessed to welcome their wisdom into our reading when we access the commentaries that were the fruit of their lectio. The monastic movement grew in the fertile soil of lectio divina. The daily, ordered life of the monks was (and is) centered upon spiritual reading of Scripture.

Can ordinary women in the twenty-first century find spiritual nourishment and new life in this age-old practice of holy men?

We can.

There are five steps in the pattern, five distinct movements that will direct the way we travel through our days. A meditation engages the mind, using reason to search for knowledge in the message. The prayer is the movement of the heart towards God, a beseeching on behalf of the soul. The contemplation elevates the mind and suspends it in God's presence. Finally, the action is the way we live our lives as gift of charity towards others. It's a tall order, but it's the very best way to live.

Let's take a careful look at each step.

Pope Benedict writes, "It opens with the reading (lectio) of a text, which leads to a desire to understand its true content: what does the biblical text say in itself (Verbum Dominus, 87). This is where we explore the literary genre of the text, the characters we meet in the story, and the objective meaning intended by the author.

"Next comes meditation (meditatio), which asks: what does the biblical text say to us?" (DV, 87). Prayerfully we ponder what personal message the text holds for each of us and what effect that message should have on our lives.

"Following this comes prayer (oratio), which asks the question: what do we say to the Lord in response to his word? Prayer, as petition, intercession, thanksgiving and praise, is the primary way by which the word transforms us" (DV, 87). How do we respond to His Word? We ask Him what He desires of us. We ask Him for the strength and grace to do His will. Moved by His mercy, we give him thanks and praise.

 The fourth act is "contemplation (contemplatio), during which we take up, as a gift from God, his own way of seeing and judging reality, and ask ourselves what conversion of mind, heart and life is the Lord asking of us?" Here, reflect on how God has conveyed His love for us in the day's Scripture. Recognize the beauty of His gifts and the goodness of His mercy and rest in that. Let God light you from within and look out on the world in a new way because you have been transformed by the process of prayerful Scripture study.

Finally, the whole point of this time we've taken from our day is to get up from the reading and go live the Gospel. Actio is where we make an act of our wills and resolve to bring the text to life in our lives. This is our fiat. "The process of lectio divina is not concluded until it arrives at action (actio), which moves the believer to make his or her life a gift for others in charity.

"We find the supreme synthesis and fulfillment of this process in the Mother of God. For every member of the faithful Mary is the model of docile acceptance of God's word, for she 'kept all these things, pondering them in her heart' " (Lk 2:19; cf. 2:51) (DV, 87).

Together, this Advent, we will endeavor to engage in lectio divina every day. We've created pages for your time of prayer, and we've created pages for your active time. We want this book to come alive in your hands, to bring you a spiritual springtime. Try to take the time each day to dig deep, but if you have to cut your time short, don't be discouraged. Ask the Blessed Mother to help you find pockets throughout the day to re-engage. Pray the parts you can, and trust the Holy Spirit to water it well in your soul. Know that God can do loaves and fishes miracles with your small parcels of time, if only you are willing to offer Him what you have. Before Advent gets swallowed with the ordinary to-to lists of seasonal hustle, sit in prayer and see how you can tune your heart to the beat of the Lord's, and ensure that the best gift you give this season is your life, given for others in charity.

ELIZABETH FOSS

first the pray

Come Holy Spirit, fill the hearts of your faithful
and kindle in them the fire of your love.
Send forth your Spirit and they shall be created.
And You shall renew the face of the earth.
O, God, who by the light of the Holy Spirit,
did instruct the hearts of the faithful,
grant that by the same Holy Spirit we may be truly wise
and ever enjoy His consolations, Through Christ Our Lord,

Amen.

LECTIO

What is the objective meaning of the text?

Who do I encounter here and what do they say?

What is the how, the where, the when & the why?

MEDITATIO

What does the biblical text say to me?

What personal message does the text have for me?

What effect does the text have on my life?

ORATIO

What do I say to the Lord in response to His word?

What does the Lord want for me? How do I ask for grace? What is my song of of thanks for His gifts & praise for His glory?

CONTEMPLATIO

How does God see and judge reality? What conversion of mind, heart, and life is He asking of me today?

How has He conveyed His love for me in today's scripture?

Where is the beauty of His gifts and the goodness of His mercy?

How will I make my life a gift for others in charity?
What does God want me to do today?

TASKS & TO DOS

MEALS TO NOURISH

GIVING & PREPARING

KEEPING HOME

ACTIO

KINDNESS TO MYSELF

How did I progress in living the Word today?

Saturday, December 2
SCRIPTURE MEMORY

Today is a day to rest and be grateful. Take some time to look over your journaling from the week, to read a little more, to catch up on days when you didn't have as much time as you would have liked.

Spend a few moments looking carefully at our memory verses, to burn the image into your brain. Then write them yourself on the weekly planning page and read them again and again when you refer to the tasks of the your weekly to-dos.

If there is a child in your life, teach these words to him or her. let Advent be hidden in their hearts. The Scripture memorized will serve that child for a lifetime. This memory work is a gift, a legacy. Hiding the Word of God in the heart of child is stocking her soul with saving grace. Together, take on this joyful endeavor. We're right there with you.

Memorizing Scripture makes it our own. When we commit it to our hearts, we always have it to carry wherever we go. This week, remember that the Lord will strengthen you to the end. It's a journey, and He's taking it with you.

1 Corinthians 1: 8-9

He will also strengthen you to the end, so that you may be blameless on the day of our Lord Jesus Christ. God is faithful; by him you were called into the fellowship of his Son, Jesus Christ our Lord.

God is faithful

1 CORINTHIANS 1:8-9

First Week of Advent

Sunday, December 3
FIRST SUNDAY OF ADVENT

MARK 13:33-37

Beware, keep alert; for you do not know when the time will come. It is like a man going on a journey, when he leaves home and puts his slaves in charge, each with his work, and commands the doorkeeper to be on the watch. Therefore, keep awake—for you do not know when the master of the house will come, in the evening, or at midnight, or at cockcrow, or at dawn, or else he may find you asleep when he comes suddenly. And what I say to you I say to all: Keep awake.

1 CORINTHIANS 1:3-9

Grace to you and peace from God our Father and the Lord Jesus Christ. I give thanks to my God always for you because of the grace of God that has been given you in Christ Jesus, for in every way you have been enriched in him, in speech and knowledge of every kind— just as the testimony of Christ has been strengthened among you— so that you are not lacking in any spiritual gift as you wait for the revealing of our Lord Jesus Christ. He will also strengthen you to the end, so that you may be blameless on the day of our Lord Jesus Christ. God is faithful; by him you were called into the fellowship of his Son, Jesus Christ our Lord.

FOR FURTHER READING

ISAIAH 63:16B-17, 19B; 64:2-7

"Light one candle for hope, one bright candle for hope..."
The notes ring out, sweet and clear as the youngest lights the first candle on our dining table Advent wreath. For Christians whose rhythms are matched to the liturgical calendar, it is a new year, bright with hope. Everything sparkles with promise: the promise of Christmas. It's right around the corner.

No, really. This year, the time truly is short. It's the shortest Advent can ever be. What does that mean for those of us who are waiting? In terms of the workaday world, it means there are 21 shopping days until Christmas. In terms of the liturgical calendar, it means there are 21 days until we celebrate the solemnity of Jesus' birth. In terms of the second coming of the Son of God, it means that we are reminded by the short season of this year's Advent that the time is coming and we might be surprised by how short the wait really is.

Jesus warns us all to be watchful. He doesn't want us to be caught by surprise. Remember though, he uttered these words two thousand years ago. People have been waiting a long time. We might have Him in our midst in just a few short weeks. Or we might need to be really patient, as patient as the generations who have lived—and—died waiting in hope before us.

What will we do while being patient? For the next three weeks, most of us will shop and wrap and bake and busy ourselves with countless to-do lists in order to make merry for the people we love.

But what will we do with our souls while waiting for the Master to arrive?

Saint Paul offers us an idea that a stretches beyond Christmas. Let us be patient in our wait, and let us also be appreciative. Thank God for the gift of faith, for the grace of knowing Him. And when the work of this wait wearies, let the understanding that grace is yours be a sustaining strength.

While we wait of the coming of the Lord, keep believing. With God's grace, Christ makes us strong in our faith until the end (V.8). While we keep vigil, the lamp of faith stays lit because God sustains our faith. Even if you struggle with doubt, even if you wrestle with wondering if it's all true, that glimmer of light flickers still (that's why it's a wrestle), and if you ask Him, He gives the flame more oxygen. God animates perseverance.

In a twist of irony worthy of Dickens, twenty-first century Decembers are quite possibly the most difficult time of the year for women to persevere in hope and faith. When the secularism of the season seeps into our souls and the wait starts to feel like work and worry, it's easy to be discouraged. What is all this bustle about? Why are we frenzied in our quest for Family Channel movie moments? Why does Christmas feel like the pursuit of perfect presents? This wait isn't really about looking around corners for magical moments when the gentle snow falls on exquisitely wrapped gifts and everyone has two mittens that match and no one's nose runs.

It's about making room in your heart for your God, so that He overcomes you with Himself.

It's about a God who humbled Himself to be born in a stable, to live a life of service, and to die bloodied on a cross in order to rescue us from our selfish sinfulness. The wait is about a God who perseveres in hope for our salvation.

Because God is faithful.

When God calls us into a relationship, He causes us to remain in Him. In this moment, we sit in the presence of God in His Word.

He speaks into our souls. The mere fact that that is happening assures us that He wants us. We are called by God into an eternal relationship with Him, and He will keep us there, safely, if we choose to nurture that faith. Slow down and seek Him.

God gives us the freedom to keep responding to Him, especially in the busyness of this season. There is hope in His call. Further, there is the assurance that while we are on the watch we will not be lacking for any spiritual gift. He will provide. Just stay awake! Be alert and cooperate with the grace that He assures. God is faithful, and you are called by Him to become more and more like Him.

Beginning today.

ELIZABETH FOSS

THE WAIT IS ABOUT A GOD WHO PERSEVERES IN HOPE FOR OUR SALVATION.

ELIZABETH FOSS

Come Holy Spirit, fill the hearts of your faithful
and kindle in them the fire of your love.
Send forth your Spirit and they shall be created.
And You shall renew the face of the earth.
O, God, who by the light of the Holy Spirit,
did instruct the hearts of the faithful,
grant that by the same Holy Spirit we may be truly wise
and ever enjoy His consolations, Through Christ Our Lord,
Amen.

LECTIO

What is the objective meaning of the text?

Who do I encounter here and what do they say?

What is the how, the where, the when & the why?

MEDITATIO

What does the biblical text say to me?

What personal message does the text have for me?

What effect does the text have on my life?

ORATIO

What do I say to the Lord in response to His word?

What does the Lord want for me? How do I ask for grace? What is my song of of thanks for His gifts & praise for His glory?

CONTEMPLATIO

How does God see and judge reality? What conversion of mind, heart, and life is He asking of me today?

How has He conveyed His love for me in today's scripture?

Where is the beauty of His gifts and the goodness of His mercy?

How will I make my life a gift for others in charity?
What does God want me to do today?

TASKS & TO DOS

MEALS TO NOURISH

GIVING & PREPARING

KEEPING HOME

ACTIO

KINDNESS TO MYSELF

How did I progress in living the Word today?

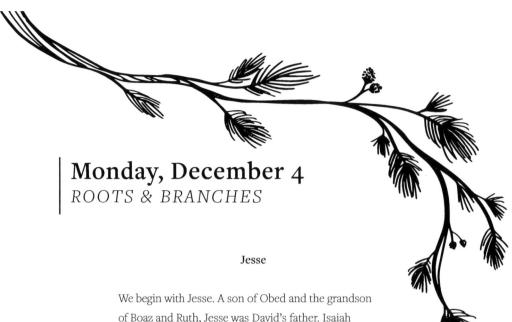

Monday, December 4
ROOTS & BRANCHES

Jesse

We begin with Jesse. A son of Obed and the grandson
of Boaz and Ruth, Jesse was David's father. Isaiah
would prophesy that the Messiah would come from
the "root of Jesse" (Isaiah 11:1, 10). Jesse came from a
prominent family, but he was mostly unknown—leading
a quiet, hidden life as the father of eight sons. (On
second thought, life with eight sons probably wasn't
all that quiet.) Unexceptional on his own merit, Jesse's
righteousness, still being realized today, was entirely
the work of God. Our focus isn't on Jesse; it's on God
at work in and through Jesse and the generations that
followed him. Salvation history unfolds one "yes" at a
time and today we consider the sturdy root of Jesse.

ISAIAH 11:1-10

A shoot shall come out from the stump of Jesse,
  and a branch shall grow out of his roots.
The spirit of the Lord shall rest on him,
  the spirit of wisdom and understanding,
  the spirit of counsel and might,
  the spirit of knowledge and the fear of the Lord.
 His delight shall be in the fear of the Lord.
He shall not judge by what his eyes see,
  or decide by what his ears hear;
but with righteousness he shall judge the poor,
  and decide with equity for the meek of the earth;
he shall strike the earth with the rod of his mouth,
  and with the breath of his lips he shall kill the wicked.
Righteousness shall be the belt around his waist,
  and faithfulness the belt around his loins.
 The wolf shall live with the lamb,
  the leopard shall lie down with the kid,
the calf and the lion and the fatling together,
  and a little child shall lead them.
The cow and the bear shall graze,
  their young shall lie down together;
  and the lion shall eat straw like the ox.
The nursing child shall play over the hole of the asp,
  and the weaned child shall put its hand on the adder's den.
They will not hurt or destroy
  on all my holy mountain;
for the earth will be full of the knowledge of the Lord
  as the waters cover the sea.
On that day the root of Jesse shall stand as a signal to the peoples; the nations shall inquire of him, and his dwelling shall be glorious.

FOR FURTHER READING

JEREMIAH 33:14-16

ROMANS 15:7-13

Without warning, nervous laughter bubbled up and overflowed into my phone. "You applied for a job where?" I asked between halted breaths.

It was an ordinary fall day, and my husband called to tell me something I'd heard many times during this long season of underemployment: he applied for a job. Only, this position was different; it required relocation from our home in the Pacific Northwest to Alabama.

Immediately, I experienced what I can only describe as an inner knowing—a whisper from the Holy Spirit, perhaps—that this job was meant to be. While I didn't hear an audible voice, somewhere deep within I sensed that not only would my husband interview for the position, he would receive an offer as well.

I laughed long and hard at God's crazy sense of humor: the sheer absurdity of leaving everything we'd known and worked for over the course of our marriage; the life we'd built for our growing family; the idea of chasing the unknown some 2,500 miles away.

Sure enough, my husband had one telephone interview, then another, and in December, he flew across the country for a series of in-person meetings. I held down the fort at home with our young children, anxiously hanging on every word when he called to tell me how well things were going and how kind everyone was.

Despite my initial acknowledgement that God was providing for our family in amazing ways, doubt and distrust crept in. I could leave belongings behind; things weren't so important to me. I could even leave the sweet little house in which we'd raised babies. Yet the thought of leaving our beloved friends, family, and community—the safety net of people we'd woven into the fabric of our lives—to follow God's call ... I spent many tears and sleepless nights begging God to provide in a way that didn't rip me away from my comfort zone.

The job offer came. My husband was excited. I was scared to death. We talked. We prayed. I begged God for peace amidst the storm of my emotions. I remembered Pope Benedict XVI's words: We are not called to comfort—we are called to greatness. And then, one day, in an act of the will, I offered a hard-fought "yes" concerning our move. A wave of peace unlike anything I'd experienced in the tumultuous days prior swept over me. God's light shone through the cracked window of my obedience, ready to illuminate the next season of our lives.

Sacred Scripture sings of individuals who said, "yes" to the LORD. Abraham, Sarah, Isaac, Jacob, Jesse, David, Joseph, and Mary—there's a long list. None were obliged to obey. God speaks into the quiet of our hearts, awaiting a response, never forcing our assent.

Upon reflection, I'm grateful that we followed God's call to Alabama. It was there that we met exceptional people who showed us great love and generosity. We prioritized relationships over results, being over doing, and community over productivity. We opened our hearts to life again, conceiving and birthing our fifth child. It was a time of great fruitfulness, which I count entirely as a blessing from Almighty God.

As His disciples, Jesus asks us, "Who do you say that I am?" Sometimes, we proclaim with Saint Peter, "You are the LORD!" We obey with great faith and trust, as Jesse did. Other times, we suffer from spiritual amnesia. Like the Israelites, we forget God's constant provision and mercy. We forget that He is God and we are not, believing we can save ourselves by forging our own path. Yet it is when we finally acknowledge God's sovereignty—when we remember His desire for our eternal happiness—that we have the courage to pick up our cross and follow where He leads.

As He has countless times before, our loving Father transforms each "yes," we offer, no matter how grand or feeble, into infinitely more than we can possibly hope for or imagine.

HEATHER RENSHAW

Come Holy Spirit, fill the hearts of your faithful
and kindle in them the fire of your love.
Send forth your Spirit and they shall be created.
And You shall renew the face of the earth.
O, God, who by the light of the Holy Spirit,
did instruct the hearts of the faithful,
grant that by the same Holy Spirit we may be truly wise
and ever enjoy His consolations, Through Christ Our Lord,
Amen.

LECTIO

What is the objective meaning of the text?

Who do I encounter here and what do they say?

What is the how, the where, the when & the why?

MEDITATIO

What does the biblical text say to me?

What personal message does the text have for me?

What effect does the text have on my life?

ORATIO

What do I say to the Lord in response to His word?

What does the Lord want for me? How do I ask for grace? What is my song of of thanks for His gifts & praise for His glory?

CONTEMPLATIO

How does God see and judge reality? What conversion of mind, heart, and life is He asking of me today?

How has He conveyed His love for me in today's scripture?

Where is the beauty of His gifts and the goodness of His mercy?

How will I make my life a gift for others in charity?
What does God want me to do today?

TASKS & TO DOS

MEALS TO NOURISH

GIVING & PREPARING

KEEPING HOME

ACTIO

KINDNESS TO MYSELF

How did I progress in living the Word today?

Tuesday, December 5
ROOTS & BRANCHES

Moses

Moses holds a mighty place in salvation history. He
was a deliverer, lawgiver, and mediator for the people
of Israel. The greatest of all prophets, Moses spoke to
God on behalf of his people and spoke to the people for
God. His friendship with the Lord was deep and true and
intimate.

Whenever we contemplate our faith, we find mystery.
Our faith is rich with mysteries—truths we know and
we take deep into our hearts, but truths we cannot fully
understand or explain. When we sit here in silence with
Moses and see the bush that is ablaze but not consumed,
we acknowledge that God can and does dwell in the
supernatural. God showed Moses—and He shows
us—that He is firmly in control of the forces of nature.
We look on in fear and wonder. A God who lights this
bush on fire but does not let it burn is a God who will
transcend natural order live among us, and then to die
and rise to new life. He dwelt in the womb of a virgin.
He is truly present in the bread and the wine. He is a
mighty Lord and the Master of the universe.

EXODUS 3:1-12

Moses at the Burning Bush

Moses was keeping the flock of his father-in-law Jethro, the priest of Midian; he led his flock beyond the wilderness, and came to Horeb, the mountain of God. There the angel of the Lord appeared to him in a flame of fire out of a bush; he looked, and the bush was blazing, yet it was not consumed. Then Moses said, "I must turn aside and look at this great sight, and see why the bush is not burned up." When the Lord saw that he had turned aside to see, God called to him out of the bush, "Moses, Moses!" And he said, "Here I am." Then he said, "Come no closer! Remove the sandals from your feet, for the place on which you are standing is holy ground." He said further, "I am the God of your father, the God of Abraham, the God of Isaac, and the God of Jacob." And Moses hid his face, for he was afraid to look at God.

Then the Lord said, "I have observed the misery of my people who are in Egypt; I have heard their cry on account of their taskmasters. Indeed, I know their sufferings, and I have come down to deliver them from the Egyptians, and to bring them up out of that land to a good and broad land, a land flowing with milk and honey, to the country of the Canaanites, the Hittites, the Amorites, the Perizzites, the Hivites, and the Jebusites. The cry of the Israelites has now come to me; I have also seen how the Egyptians oppress them. So come, I will send you to Pharaoh to bring my people, the Israelites, out of Egypt." But Moses said to God, "Who am I that I should go to Pharaoh, and bring the Israelites out of Egypt?" He said, "I will be with you; and this shall be the sign for you that it is I who sent you: when you have brought the people out of Egypt, you shall worship God on this mountain."

FOR FURTHER READING

EXODUS 3:13-22

HEBREWS 12:29

Sometimes, when we read the Old Testament, it can seem tedious and confusing (do I honestly need to know the length and width of ALL the temple curtains?). Other times, such as in today's reading from the book of Exodus, the story has roots that reach right down through the ground, travel forward in time through dust and dirt to the life of Jesus Christ, and reach ahead again, encircling our very hearts.

The life of Moses is often seen as a prefigurement of the Annunciation, Incarnation, and the Holy Eucharist. It's one of many Biblical examples showing that it is God who seeks us, purifies us, and sends us forth to participate in the mission of His Kingdom.

In this passage, God seeks Moses in the burning of the bush. He waits for Moses to take notice and then calls him by name. Moses isn't just a tool to God; God loves him deeply and seeks his willful participation in salvation history. Once God has Moses' attention, he shows him in the burning of the bush that His love is blazing but it will not not consume. It is the purifying love of God, His very grace set upon our hearts to remove all trace of sinfulness. Once Moses has experienced this purification, God gives him both the instructions and the courage to complete his mission of rescuing the Israelite people from slavery.

Again, hundreds of years later, when the angel Gabriel visits Mary, he seeks her and calls her by name. He brings the news that she has a special mission in bringing the Messiah to the Israelite people, and seeks her consent. Fortunately for all of creation, she has always had within her the desire to unite her will to that of our Heavenly Father. After she consents to mother the Savior, Mary is overshadowed by the Holy Spirit and begins her holy role as the Virgin Mother. Her fiat, the wonderful and eternal yes to God, allows Christ to come into the world and free us from the slavery of sin.

The Blessed Virgin and Moses were unique in their time. Each of us, however, has the undeniably precious gift of God seeking us every day in the Consecration at Mass. We too, humble like Mary and sinful like Moses, are sought by our very own Creator. When, in a state of grace, we receive the Holy Eucharist, we consent again and again to God's purifying flame. It is a blazing fire that burns away what we don't need but that leaves the essence of our true self, the self that longs to be most closely united with Christ, as Mary was. At the end of the Mass, the priest sends us forth to continue with the mission of evangelization. Simple though we may see ourselves, just like Moses and Mary, God has given us a completely unique role in His Kingdom. We, too, can be an example of what true freedom looks like.

Have you been still enough to hear God calling your name? It's critical that we make time every day to pray in silence, to turn off the noise around us so that we notice the presence of God in our lives.

Have you experienced this sort of blazing fire in your life? Saint Paul refers to God as a consuming fire (Hebrews 12:29). It's not always a pleasant experience to have habits and vices stripped from us, but our Heavenly Father's fire will only burn off the unnecessary evil in our life. No matter how painful, He will not consume us. He made us in His image and loves us so tenderly, so dearly, as a father loves every freckle on his daughter's nose and every hair on her head.

Have you taken up the mission God has given you in your life? Are you fulfilling the tasks set before you, no matter how humble, no matter how difficult? If that's a struggle for you, take heart and begin again today by trying to hear God's voice, and by frequent reception of the sacraments. The more we listen and are purified, the clearer our mission will become.

MICAELA DARR

Come Holy Spirit, fill the hearts of your faithful
and kindle in them the fire of your love.
Send forth your Spirit and they shall be created.
And You shall renew the face of the earth.
O, God, who by the light of the Holy Spirit,
did instruct the hearts of the faithful,
grant that by the same Holy Spirit we may be truly wise
and ever enjoy His consolations, Through Christ Our Lord,
Amen.

LECTIO

What is the objective meaning of the text?

Who do I encounter here and what do they say?

What is the how, the where, the when & the why?

MEDITATIO

What does the biblical text say to me?

What personal message does the text have for me?

What effect does the text have on my life?

ORATIO

What do I say to the Lord in response to His word?

What does the Lord want for me? How do I ask for grace? What is my song of of thanks for His gifts & praise for His glory?

CONTEMPLATIO

How does God see and judge reality? What conversion of mind, heart, and life is He asking of me today?

How has He conveyed His love for me in today's scripture?

Where is the beauty of His gifts and the goodness of His mercy?

How will I make my life a gift for others in charity?
What does God want me to do today?

TASKS & TO DOS

MEALS TO NOURISH

GIVING & PREPARING

KEEPING HOME

KINDNESS TO MYSELF

ACTIO

How did I progress in living the Word today?

Wednesday, December 6
ROOTS & BRANCHES

Gideon

Gideon was a prophet whose name means "mighty warrior." God called to Gideon and asked him to defeat the Midianites and save Israel. Despite his faith, Gideon had his doubts; he was insecure and worried about whether he was capable of doing what God called him to do. Gideon set out a fleece and asked for a sign and begged for God to prove Himself before he would step out in faith to live his vocation. He wanted God to overcome the natural and leave a supernatural sign: he wanted dew on the fleece he laid on the threshing floor, but a dry floor all around it. Then he wanted the fleece to be dry and the floor to be wet with dew. He was not easily persuaded.

Saint Ambrose saw the dew as the Divine Word, sent from heaven to speak into Gideon's heart. Saint Augustine saw Christ as the "sweetness of the dew," and so, Gideon's fleece, which absorbed the dew, is like the womb of the Mother of God. She received Christ in her own body and she bore Him into the world. She was a living, breathing sign of the miraculous things that God will do; she was also a living, breathing example to us of stepping out in faith, even without a sign, in order to answer God's call.

JUDGES 6:36-40

Then Gideon said to God, "In order to see whether you will deliver Israel by my hand, as you have said, I am going to lay a fleece of wool on the threshing floor; if there is dew on the fleece alone, and it is dry on all the ground, then I shall know that you will deliver Israel by my hand, as you have said." And it was so. When he rose early next morning and squeezed the fleece, he wrung enough dew from the fleece to fill a bowl with water. Then Gideon said to God, "Do not let your anger burn against me, let me speak one more time; let me, please, make trial with the fleece just once more; let it be dry only on the fleece, and on all the ground let there be dew." And God did so that night. It was dry on the fleece only, and on all the ground there was dew.

FOR FURTHER READING

ROMANS 8:24-28

ALL OF JUDGES

A few days after Mother's Day 2016, I decided I'd better take a pregnancy test. I didn't really expect it to be positive. My cycle had been out of whack, and a doctor had even suggested I was entering perimenopause.

Besides, only months earlier I'd cleared out all things baby and had stopped pining for another little one. It was time to focus on this season of motherhood and to celebrate milestones like no longer being in the business of hazardous waste removal.

Well, bring on the poop. I was pregnant.

When I saw those two pink lines, I started to cry. For the first time, my tears following a positive pregnancy test weren't out of joy but stemmed from uncertainty and fear.

I felt a lot like Gideon then. I wasn't sure I could do what God was asking of me.

After all, I had prayed for another baby, but when it didn't happen, I oh-so-bravely accepted God's will. Now, He was hurling a curveball in my direction, and I wasn't sure I had what it took to catch it. It didn't help that I was plagued with all-day nausea during the entire pregnancy and ended up in the hospital because of dehydration and preterm contractions.

But as God so often does, He gifted me with divine nudges that it was going to be okay.

Just two days after the positive pregnancy test, my oldest child waltzed into the kitchen and said out of the blue, "Can we adopt? I know you're too old to have a baby [*Ha! I'll show her!*], but I really want a baby in the house, and I could help so much!"

And this teen of mine has been an invaluable help – holding her baby brother, changing his diaper, playing with him when my hands are full with other tasks. My husband showered me with love and support and showed daily excitement about the little wonder growing inside of me when I couldn't because of nausea, fear, or exhaustion. When I lamented my current lack of baby paraphernalia, a generous friend immediately started listing all of the things she had to share with me.

My mom gently reminded me that one of my best friends – my younger brother – was also a surprise. She discovered she was pregnant after she'd been diagnosed with some health problems, and she was scared, too, but my brother has proven to be a huge blessing to us all, and he truly is one of the most caring, unselfish people we know.

Then after an exhausting but beautiful labor, my baby Charlie was placed in my arms, and I wondered why I'd ever doubted God at all. I can do hard things, I thought. I'd just spent my final weeks of pregnancy in Advent waiting not only for Christ, but for my own baby. And here he was - joy personified.

Today is the Feast of Saint Nicholas. My children will wake and run to their stockings in hopes of finding tiny treats and trinkets. What would happen if their stockings were empty? If there was no sign of a treasure even after their hands plunged deeply into the oversized socks? I expect my younger children might cry. Isn't that what I have done when I've been faced with the unexpected?

But what did Mary do? Mary, unlike dear Gideon, always trusted her Father. Always. Even when she was scared, confused, or pierced with a sword of sorrow. We're called to do the same - even if it takes a lifetime to learn to do so.

What are you afraid of at this very moment? Sometimes what God asks of us is only suffering. It's only human to ask God for a sign when you're hurting and feel scared, but you may be met with radio silence. You may not have your own bone-dry fleece or dew-speckled ground. What then? Will you still answer God's call in faith and go where He leads you? Are we willing to lead lives marked by joy and serenity regardless of our circumstances and whether or not we can recognize God's hand in our lives? That's what it takes to be a saint, my dear sister, to trust in Our Father even when there are no clear signs or answers and to believe in His goodness when life doesn't feel so good at all.

God may lose battles, but He wins the war. Advent is a season of hope. It's also a season that demands patience--not only in the crowded malls but in your hearts as well. As Saint Ignatius of Loyola said, "In a time of desolation, never forsake the good resolutions you made in better times. Strive to remain patient--a virtue contrary to the troubles that harass you-- and remember you will be consoled."

KATE WICKER

THAT'S WHAT IT TAKES TO BE A SAINT, MY DEAR SISTER, TO TRUST IN OUR FATHER EVEN WHEN THERE ARE NO CLEAR SIGNS OR ANSWERS

KATE WICKER

Come Holy Spirit, fill the hearts of your faithful
and kindle in them the fire of your love.
Send forth your Spirit and they shall be created.
And You shall renew the face of the earth.
O, God, who by the light of the Holy Spirit,
did instruct the hearts of the faithful,
grant that by the same Holy Spirit we may be truly wise
and ever enjoy His consolations, Through Christ Our Lord,
Amen.

LECTIO

What is the objective meaning of the text?

Who do I encounter here and what do they say?

What is the how, the where, the when & the why?

MEDITATIO

What does the biblical text say to me?

What personal message does the text have for me?

What effect does the text have on my life?

ORATIO

What do I say to the Lord in response to His word?

What does the Lord want for me? How do I ask for grace? What is my song of of thanks for His gifts & praise for His glory?

CONTEMPLATIO

How does God see and judge reality? What conversion of mind, heart, and life is He asking of me today?

How has He conveyed His love for me in today's scripture?

Where is the beauty of His gifts and the goodness of His mercy?

How will I make my life a gift for others in charity?
What does God want me to do today?

TASKS & TO DOS

MEALS TO NOURISH

GIVING & PREPARING

ACTIO

KEEPING HOME

KINDNESS TO MYSELF

How did I progress in living the Word today?

Thursday, December 7
ROOTS & BRANCHES

Samuel

Someone wanted Samuel, begged for him, beseeched the Lord with fervent prayers for him. The fruit of those prayers was the fruit of Hannah's womb. Hannah, Samuel's mother, was a faithful woman who, when God answered her prayer, returned her son to the temple and dedicated him to God. There, under the care of Eli, he grew into a man of honor, who loved God's people. "The word of the Lord was rare in those days; visions were not widespread" (1 Samuel 3:1). But God spoke insistently to Samuel. As he grew, the Lord's revelations, carefully stewarded by Samuel, established for him a reputation for trustworthiness. Samuel's horn was filled with the holy oil of anointing, and God sent him to Bethlehem to anoint David, Jesse's youngest son, to be the successor of Saul. Later, Samuel would also be a protector, a holy prophet who befriended David and sheltered him against Saul's rage. Samuel's life is a testimony to God's faithfulness and to His generosity when He hears and answers our prayers.

1 SAMUEL 1:9-18

After they had eaten and drunk at Shiloh, Hannah rose and presented herself before the Lord. Now Eli the priest was sitting on the seat beside the doorpost of the temple of the Lord. 10 She was deeply distressed and prayed to the Lord, and wept bitterly. She made this vow: "O Lord of hosts, if only you will look on the misery of your servant, and remember me, and not forget your servant, but will give to your servant a male child, then I will set him before you as a Nazirite until the day of his death. He shall drink neither wine nor intoxicants and no razor shall touch his head." As she continued praying before the Lord, Eli observed her mouth. Hannah was praying silently; only her lips moved, but her voice was not heard; therefore Eli thought she was drunk. So Eli said to her, "How long will you make a drunken spectacle of yourself? Put away your wine." But Hannah answered, "No, my lord, I am a woman deeply troubled; I have drunk neither wine nor strong drink, but I have been pouring out my soul before the Lord. Do not regard your servant as a worthless woman, for I have been speaking out of my great anxiety and vexation all this time." Then Eli answered, "Go in peace; the God of Israel grant the petition you have made to him." And she said, "Let your servant find favor in your sight." Then the woman went to her quarters, ate and drank with her husband, and her countenance was sad no longer.

FOR FURTHER READING

1 SAMUEL 1-3 (EARLY LIFE OF SAMUEL)

1 SAMUEL 10 (ANOINTING OF SAUL)

1 SAMUEL 16:1-13 (ANOINTING OF DAVID)

Hannah's heart was so broken with the grief of longing that her deepest prayers looked to the holy eyes of Eli like someone who had too much wine. What burning embarrassment must have crept into Hannah's face when Eli approached her with that claim! Yet Hannah was unashamed to lay not only her grief, but her great hope, before God and his servant Eli, and to trust that they would hear the cries of her heart.

I certainly can relate to the notion of being nearly drunk with grief, to being seized with longings so deep that they spring from my heart as a prayer of jumbled words, hot tears, and unspeakable pain. But far too often, when my heart is hurting, my faith can stagnate right there, and I can forget that my call is to follow Hannah's example and be a woman of hope even in my grief.

It is Hannah's hope that lifts her prayer up beyond pleading to worship, rising up like incense in the temple that day. It is hope that makes the difference between the prayer that opens our eyes to redemption and the prayer that forgets that help is on its way. It is hope that makes our prayers bold enough for us to defend them even when they make us look a little crazy. It is hope that lets us open our hands for the answer and keep them open, holding all the grace that is poured into them when God responds loosely enough that it rises back up to Him again as praise.

I have often wondered just how Hannah did it, kept that promise to give her precious, sought after Samuel back to God after she had waited and begged for so long and finally received her heart's greatest desire. What I see now is that it is Hannah's hope that allows her to hold both her pain and her joy loosely, letting God do as He wishes with both of them. Because Hannah is a woman of hope, she believes in the goodness of God, and she trusts that redemption comes to us in all things. She wholeheartedly lives the oft-repeated modern mantra that "all is grace."

And when all is grace, we can wait out our pain and longing in hope. When all is grace, we can give God back our answered prayers in faith. When all is grace, we can see salvation coming in glimpses and flashes, and take up our place in its story. When all is grace, we can be drunk with grief and bold with hope all at once. Because this is just what salvation is: the cradle and the cross, the grave and the stone rolled away, the dark days before a Savior and the lit up skies of "Hosanna in the highest." Hannah's hope is our reminder that when we pray, this is the filter that turns the drunken nonsense of our humanity into holy hope of our eternal faith.

The boy who is the answer to those broken, hopeful prayers, offered back to God by Hannah, becomes the priest who anoints Saul king at the pleading of Israel. He puts into the motion the answer to another prayer, the prayer of the people for God's blessing, for God's rescue—their prayer to be saved. And even though their demand for a king is a truly broken, drunken prayer, it is a prayer of hope, and prayer that God can save them if he chooses to.

The oil of anointing that Samuel pours over Saul eventually drips down to David, who rises up to become the king who will become a beacon for Israel, a light in the darkness, a forbearer of the Good News of our salvation in Jesus Christ.

We are all the pray-ers of broken prayers. We are all begging at the throne of grace to be saved. If we can all be hopeful that God knows the heart of those prayers and will answer them with the compassion that leads to our eternal redemption, then we can all stand in the tableau of salvation history beside Hannah, bold-hearted and brave. Because we are broken-hearted, but we are believers, and we see salvation on the horizon.

COLLEEN MITCHELL

*Come Holy Spirit, fill the hearts of your faithful
and kindle in them the fire of your love.
Send forth your Spirit and they shall be created.
And You shall renew the face of the earth.
O, God, who by the light of the Holy Spirit,
did instruct the hearts of the faithful,
grant that by the same Holy Spirit we may be truly wise
and ever enjoy His consolations, Through Christ Our Lord,
Amen.*

LECTIO

What is the objective meaning of the text?

Who do I encounter here and what do they say?

What is the how, the where, the when & the why?

MEDITATIO

What does the biblical text say to me?

What personal message does the text have for me?

What effect does the text have on my life?

ORATIO

What do I say to the Lord in response to His word?

What does the Lord want for me? How do I ask for grace?
What is my song of of thanks for His gifts & praise for His glory?

CONTEMPLATIO

How does God see and judge reality? What conversion of mind, heart, and life is He asking of me today?

How has He conveyed His love for me in today's scripture?

Where is the beauty of His gifts and the goodness of His mercy?

How will I make my life a gift for others in charity?
What does God want me to do today?

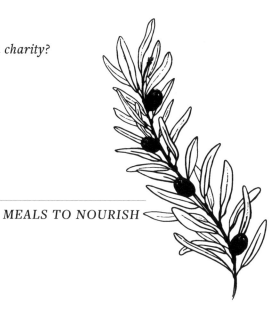

TASKS & TO DOS

MEALS TO NOURISH

GIVING & PREPARING

KEEPING HOME

KINDNESS TO MYSELF

ACTIO

How did I progress in living the Word today?

Friday, December 8
ROOTS & BRANCHES

Immaculate Conception

"Today humanity, in all the radiance of her immaculate nobility, receives its ancient beauty. The shame of sin had darkened the splendor and attraction of human nature...this nature regains in her person its ancient privileges and is fashioned according to a perfect model truly worthy of God...The reform of our nature begins today and the aged world, subjected to a wholly divine transformation, receives the first fruits of the second creation."

Saint Andrew of Crete

EPHESIANS 1:3-12

Blessed be the God and Father of our Lord Jesus Christ, who has blessed us in Christ with every spiritual blessing in the heavenly places, just as he chose us in Christ before the foundation of the world to be holy and blameless before him in love. He destined us for adoption as his children through Jesus Christ, according to the good pleasure of his will, to the praise of his glorious grace that he freely bestowed on us in the Beloved. In him we have redemption through his blood, the forgiveness of our trespasses, according to the riches of his grace that he lavished on us. With all wisdom and insight he has made known to us the mystery of his will, according to his good pleasure that he set forth in Christ, as a plan for the fullness of time, to gather up all things in him, things in heaven and things on earth. In Christ we have also obtained an inheritance, having been destined according to the purpose of him who accomplishes all things according to his counsel and will, so that we, who were the first to set our hope on Christ, might live for the praise of his glory.

CONSIDER THE READINGS FROM MASS:

GENESIS 3:9-15, 20

PSALM 98

EPHESIANS 1:3-6, 11-12

LUKE 1:26-38

Advent. It's a season of preparing and it anticipates another season, one of giving. Looking around at the world this time of year, you'd think these weeks are all about buying the right things and having them ready to give at just the right time. This season of anticipation can quickly become a season of anxiety when we lose sight of the real gift. That Gift is not one to be found in stores and it can't be bought. In fact, this Gift is not a thing, but a Person. And there's no reason to worry about the timing of this gift. God took care of every detail. Today is a day about the details.

God isn't bound by the constraint of time. He's never late in what He gives. In fact, sometimes He gives His gifts early, His timing is always perfect. Today is about a gift given in anticipation. As someone who is the least likely to keep a surprise or hold on to a gift, I smile to myself when I think of God giving this singular grace to His Mother ahead of time. That gift was the indwelling of the Holy Spirit, from the very first moment of her conception, the life of sanctifying grace—the Virgin's union with God. It was a gift given even before He worked our salvation in time.

It's a gift He has in store for all of us.

That's what's so exciting about today. It points to the gift in the manger and reminds us of what that Divine Person, who shares our flesh, means for all of us. The Immaculate Mary's destiny is that of every person of faith. What's already been realized in her is a promise of our potential. Today is a day of rejoicing and hope. What God gave her by anticipation, He offers to us by way of deliverance—a gift as well, His very life.

How fitting that we celebrate God's anticipatory gift to the Mother of God during this season of preparing! I think the timing is perfect—that we're reminded by the Church during these days of getting ready, how He prepared a dwelling for Himself. When the worry about shopping and finding that perfect earthly gift can quickly overwhelm us, it's important to pause and remember on this day of the Immaculate Conception that God gives the best gifts. This singular gift of grace was the most perfect of all gifts, not only because of Who God is, but because of who the Virgin was to become—the Ark of the New Covenant. The perfection of her humanity points to His divinity.

In these days of Advent, when you're tempted to look to the consumer world for examples of Pinterest and Insta-perfect giving and preparing, let today be a reminder of the true example of what it really means to prepare in order to give. Let's remind ourselves how, in anticipation of giving the gift of Himself to the world, He prepared a place, a beautiful dwelling, full of grace— the Immaculate heart of a humble Virgin.

She received the first fruits. That means those fruits are promised to us as well! So let's not burden ourselves this Advent with worry about timing, because we know that God's timing is perfect. We'll probably forget something here or there. We may even be late or miss opportunities to enter into the worldly celebration of the season. That's fine. It doesn't matter how little or how much you do. All these things pass. God's already given everything needful. He's prepared everything for us. The gifts of God are neither early nor belated. Let today be a lesson to us of the one thing needful during these weeks of Advent and always—that we prepare a place for Him in our hearts. Our model, rich in the fullness of His grace, is set before us and she's here to help us. With a firm resolve, let's get back to this season of preparing, focused on what it really means to make ready and give.

KATHERINE JOHNSON

Come Holy Spirit, fill the hearts of your faithful
and kindle in them the fire of your love.
Send forth your Spirit and they shall be created.
And You shall renew the face of the earth.
O, God, who by the light of the Holy Spirit,
did instruct the hearts of the faithful,
grant that by the same Holy Spirit we may be truly wise
and ever enjoy His consolations, Through Christ Our Lord,
Amen.

LECTIO

What is the objective meaning of the text?

Who do I encounter here and what do they say?

What is the how, the where, the when & the why?

MEDITATIO

What does the biblical text say to me?

What personal message does the text have for me?

What effect does the text have on my life?

ORATIO

What do I say to the Lord in response to His word?

What does the Lord want for me? How do I ask for grace? What is my song of of thanks for His gifts & praise for His glory?

CONTEMPLATIO

How does God see and judge reality? What conversion of mind, heart, and life is He asking of me today?

How has He conveyed His love for me in today's scripture?

Where is the beauty of His gifts and the goodness of His mercy?

How will I make my life a gift for others in charity?
What does God want me to do today?

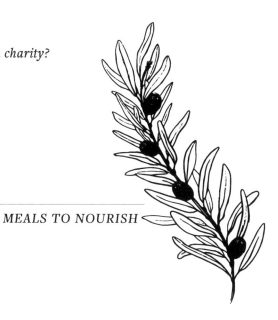

TASKS & TO DOS

MEALS TO NOURISH

GIVING & PREPARING

KEEPING HOME

ACTIO

KINDNESS TO MYSELF

How did I progress in living the Word today?

Saturday, December 9
SCRIPTURE MEMORY

Memorizing Scripture makes it our own. When we commit it to our hearts, we always have it to carry wherever we go. This week, remember that the Lord will strengthen you to the end. It's a journey, and He's taking it with you. This week, we look with love on the Prince of Peace who will make us perfectly holy in His time.

Today is a day to rest and be grateful. Take some time to look over your journaling from the week, to read a little more, to catch up on days when you didn't have as much time as you would have liked.

Spend a few moments looking carefully at our memory verse, to burn the image into your brain. Then write them yourself on the weekly planning page and read them again and again when you refer to the tasks of the your weekly to-dos.

One more thing: if there is a child in your life, teach these words to him or her. They will serve that child for a lifetime. Don't be surprised when the child memorizes more easily than you do, even when the verses are longer. This memory work is a gift, a legacy. Hiding the Word of God in the heart of child is stocking his soul with saving grace. Together, take on this joyful endeavor. We're right there with you.

1 Thessalonians 5:23

May the God of peace himself make you perfectly holy and may you entirely, spirit, soul, and body, be preserved blameless for the coming of our Lord Jesus Christ

May the GOD of peace HIMSELF make you perfectly HOLY

1 THESSALONIANS 5:23

Second Week
of Advent

Week of Sunday, December 10

SUNDAY | DECEMBER 10

MONDAY | DECEMBER 11

TUESDAY | DECEMBER 12

WEDNESDAY | DECEMBER 13

THURSDAY | DECEMBER 14

FRIDAY | DECEMBER 15

SATURDAY | DECEMBER 16

feast day celebration ideas

Second Week of Advent

to - dos

memory verse

give + prepare

1 THESSALONIANS 5:23

prayer requests

Sunday, December 10
FIRST SUNDAY OF ADVENT

MARK 1:1-8

The Proclamation of John the Baptist

The beginning of the good news of Jesus Christ, the Son of God.

As it is written in the prophet Isaiah,

"See, I am sending my messenger ahead of you,
   who will prepare your way;
the voice of one crying out in the wilderness:
   'Prepare the way of the Lord,
   make his paths straight,'"

John the baptizer appeared in the wilderness, proclaiming a baptism of repentance for the forgiveness of sins. And people from the whole Judean countryside and all the people of Jerusalem were going out to him, and were baptized by him in the river Jordan, confessing their sins. Now John was clothed with camel's hair, with a leather belt around his waist, and he ate locusts and wild honey. He proclaimed, "The one who is more powerful than I is coming after me; I am not worthy to stoop down and untie the thong of his sandals. I have baptized you with water; but he will baptize you with the Holy Spirit."

FOR FURTHER READING

2 PETER 3:8-14

ISAIAH 40:1-5, 9-11

Some days I stagger from the stove with that first cup of something hot, and I wonder how I will do the day. I look at the tasks before me—the bullet points of this vocation— and I'm blown away by how impossible it all seems. My own sense of inadequacy bubbles up to a point that I am reduced to scrolling Instagram for a few moments, as if visual evidence of other people's success in all parameters of life will somehow fuel my own. Do you ever do that? Look around the room, preoccupied with yourself, while at the same time measuring your worth against everyone else? Do you wander aimlessly through social media, exiled from your real life?

What a prophetic invitation Isaiah offers to us! The people of Israel had been wandering in exile and Isaiah invited them to return to their home. After the trials of exile, their time of salvation and hope had come. There was a tender gentleness in his tone as he gathered his flock and promised hope.

We wander, too. We drift from the freedom the Lord offers into the enslavement of our passions. We wander into sin, frankly, and we sense that we are exiled from God. There is a way back; there's a tender mercy waiting for you this Advent. Confession brings us back to our homeland and expiates our guilt. Our humility and His forgiveness anchor us in our own lives and then fuel us to live out the vision God has for those lives. It's better than anything we can see while we scroll. God waits to lead us from the sadness, to offer to us His consolation.

John the Baptist cries out in the wilderness, echoing the words of Isaiah. Their mission is the same. They both want their people to know the consolation of God. They both come to the mission as holy men who wholly know the friendship of the Lord. They know what joy intimacy with God is, and they come to that joy unencumbered by the things that weigh most of us down. They are not bound by the world's chains.

John the Baptist leapt for joy in the presence of the Lord before he was born. From the very beginning, he was joyful before the Lord. In those small beginnings and then in the simple approach to even the most basic necessities of life—what he would eat and what he would wear—John the Baptist was humble.

Both prophets were effective communicators of the call to repentance and of the Lord's consolation, because their lives were an expression of the joy of the Lord. They were humble, but they didn't hide their gifts—they lived them joyfully out loud in the world. They understood that they were uniquely called to prophecy. They were confident in their roles, and they wasted no time trumpeting their own horns. Instead, they dedicated themselves to heralding the Savior. They were joyful because they were humble.

John knew he was not fit to loosen the thongs of his Savior's sandals. He didn't exalt Himself. He didn't worry about his platform. He focused on pointing his people to Jesus. He battled neither his own sense of inadequacy nor an inflated sense of self. He was uniquely called to proclaim God; he lived that vocation with extraordinary joy. His humility burst forth in his joy.

He did not mince words when he called the people to repentance. John knew that humility and repentance would yield intimacy with Jesus. When we are humble, God consoles. When we recognize that He is the one who fuels our days—not the cup of something hot and certainly not the scroll through social media—we have enough. We are enough. We can do whatever it is God intends for us to do.

This week, put humility on your to-do list. Take some time from your busy-ness to make an honest accounting of your sins. Then, kneel before the throne of mercy. Confess your sins, and hear the words of mercy. In what is only a few moments of painful awkwardness, you will be offered the grace of humble joy. You will be given everything you need to live your vocation as God intends you to live it.

ELIZABETH FOSS

Come Holy Spirit, fill the hearts of your faithful
and kindle in them the fire of your love.
Send forth your Spirit and they shall be created.
And You shall renew the face of the earth.
O, God, who by the light of the Holy Spirit,
did instruct the hearts of the faithful,
grant that by the same Holy Spirit we may be truly wise
and ever enjoy His consolations, Through Christ Our Lord,
Amen.

LECTIO

What is the objective meaning of the text?

Who do I encounter here and what do they say?

What is the how, the where, the when & the why?

MEDITATIO

What does the biblical text say to me?

What personal message does the text have for me?

What effect does the text have on my life?

ORATIO

What do I say to the Lord in response to His word?

What does the Lord want for me? How do I ask for grace? What is my song of of thanks for His gifts & praise for His glory?

CONTEMPLATIO

How does God see and judge reality? What conversion of mind, heart, and life is He asking of me today?

How has He conveyed His love for me in today's scripture?

Where is the beauty of His gifts and the goodness of His mercy?

How will I make my life a gift for others in charity?
What does God want me to do today?

TASKS & TO DOS

MEALS TO NOURISH

GIVING & PREPARING

KEEPING HOME

A C T I O

KINDNESS TO MYSELF

How did I progress in living the Word today?

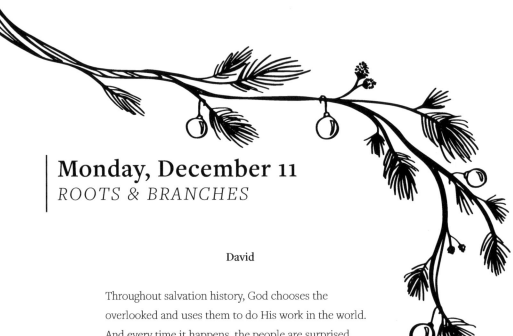

Monday, December 11
ROOTS & BRANCHES

David

Throughout salvation history, God chooses the overlooked and uses them to do His work in the world. And every time it happens, the people are surprised. Jesse offered David to the prophet as an afterthought. The young shepherd appeared before Samuel and he was ruddy, and had beautiful eyes, and was handsome (1 Samuel 16:12).

Jesse (and his other seven sons) were surprised when Samuel anointed the youngest boy. God knew that David was more than he appeared to be. God saw into the heart and soul of the man and God chose to use him—frailties and all—to be a mighty branch in the tree of the family of Jesus. Despite his mostly triumphant reign, David was a grievous sinner whose transgressions filled his later years with misery. Despite being painfully aware that he had deeply betrayed God, he returned again and again to the throne of mercy. God loved David. God sees what the world doesn't, and God judges beyond the surface, beyond the façade, well beyond the way things appear. Those beautiful eyes—windows to the soul—laid bare to the Lord the truth of the boy, and God saw in him a king who could be trusted with the lineage of salvation.

1 SAMUEL 16:1-13

The Lord said to Samuel, "How long will you grieve over Saul? I have rejected him from being king over Israel. Fill your horn with oil and set out; I will send you to Jesse the Bethlehemite, for I have provided for myself a king among his sons." Samuel said, "How can I go? If Saul hears of it, he will kill me." And the Lord said, "Take a heifer with you, and say, 'I have come to sacrifice to the Lord.' Invite Jesse to the sacrifice, and I will show you what you shall do; and you shall anoint for me the one whom I name to you." Samuel did what the Lord commanded, and came to Bethlehem. The elders of the city came to meet him trembling, and said, "Do you come peaceably?" He said, "Peaceably; I have come to sacrifice to the Lord; sanctify yourselves and come with me to the sacrifice." And he sanctified Jesse and his sons and invited them to the sacrifice. When they came, he looked on Eliab and thought, "Surely the Lord's anointed is now before the Lord." But the Lord said to Samuel, "Do not look on his appearance or on the height of his stature, because I have rejected him; for the Lord does not see as mortals see; they look on the outward appearance, but the Lord looks on the heart." Then Jesse called Abinadab, and made him pass before Samuel. He said, "Neither has the Lord chosen this one." Then Jesse made Shammah pass by. And he said, "Neither has the Lord chosen this one." Jesse made seven of his sons pass before Samuel, and Samuel said to Jesse, "The Lord has not chosen any of these." Samuel said to Jesse, "Are all your sons here?" And he said, "There remains yet the youngest, but he is keeping the sheep." And Samuel said to Jesse, "Send and bring him; for we will not sit down until he comes here." He sent and brought him in. Now he was ruddy, and had beautiful eyes, and was handsome. The Lord said, "Rise and anoint him; for this is the one." Then Samuel took the horn of oil, and anointed him in the presence of his brothers; and the spirit of the Lord came mightily upon David from that day forward. Samuel then set out and went to Ramah.

FOR FURTHER READING

1 SAMUEL 17

In my high school English classroom, I have one major objective as I try to set the tone of our community: I want this to be a place where you, my students, are seen. A space where you don't need to hide because you feel comfortable. A space where you may not like every person in the room, but you respect them. A space where we are all on the same team. If I can manage to create such a place for the 150 different backgrounds, personalities, and daily baggages that come through my door, it will be a near miracle. But I still want to try. I want the students to be seen—because what I really want is for them to feel loved.

While this is a noble goal for creating a space, the tricky opposite is often a personal objective of mine: I wish to be seen in the spaces I occupy. Am I contributing to the faculty meeting? Do I have a place at the family table? Am I present in my friendships? Is my online persona annoying or friendly? Am I seen, and how? Who's looking?

The desire to be seen—loved—is an innate trait in all of us. The trap can come, though, when we start to focus on wanting the love of all, instead of the love of a few who matter.

The fact is, there is no way you are going to please them all.

The fact is, you deserve to be seen, but some will still turn their eyes away. Or look on with disgust. Or raise their eyebrows in judgement.

That is not how God sees, "for the Lord does not see as mortals see; they look on the outward appearance, but the Lord looks on the heart" (1 Samuel 16:6). And when we sense the wayward glances of our peers--or worse, feel like nobody's watching at all-- it is so hard to remember that only one gaze really matters. If we let it, His gaze can fulfill our deep desire to be loved completely, all on its own.

How does God look at us? I usually imagine that His eyes are soft, proud, and laughing. He is the best kind of teacher: His presence demands respect, but He is warm. His look should be enough, but sometimes it isn't--I'm too concerned with the glances that everyone else is throwing (or not throwing) my way.

This is tough, ladies: have you ever felt like no one in the earthly realm is noticing you? The desire to be seen, I think, can be fueled by our fear of loneliness, a truly biting dread. Perhaps no one is noticing your hard work or efforts to be a better mom, sister, daughter, colleague, or person. It's so easy to feel like everyone else is at the big party on parade, being showered with love for their accomplishments, and you're left in the field with no recognition, keeping to the sheep alone.

Wait—but who ends up as King in that situation again?

David, an emblem of humility, didn't give a darn about who was looking at him and who wasn't. He simply persevered to finish the task in front of him, and with the Spirit of the Lord as his guide, he knew the eyes he should be seeking. As a human King, David will have his own struggles with sin and temptation later, but he understands that one pair of eyes is in a different category above all the others, and that God's gaze of approval is one worth striving for. It is no surprise to me that in a few chapters, this is the man who man understands that you can't fight Goliath if you're listening to everyone telling you you're going to fail.

In a season when so much is on display, it's reassuring to remember that only one gaze, one that looks with the heart, matters most.

KATY GREINER

Come Holy Spirit, fill the hearts of your faithful
and kindle in them the fire of your love.
Send forth your Spirit and they shall be created.
And You shall renew the face of the earth.
O, God, who by the light of the Holy Spirit,
did instruct the hearts of the faithful,
grant that by the same Holy Spirit we may be truly wise
and ever enjoy His consolations, Through Christ Our Lord,
Amen.

LECTIO

What is the objective meaning of the text?

Who do I encounter here and what do they say?

What is the how, the where, the when & the why?

MEDITATIO

What does the biblical text say to me?

What personal message does the text have for me?

What effect does the text have on my life?

ORATIO

What do I say to the Lord in response to His word?

What does the Lord want for me? How do I ask for grace? What is my song of of thanks for His gifts & praise for His glory?

CONTEMPLATIO

How does God see and judge reality? What conversion of mind, heart, and life is He asking of me today?

How has He conveyed His love for me in today's scripture?

Where is the beauty of His gifts and the goodness of His mercy?

How will I make my life a gift for others in charity?
What does God want me to do today?

TASKS & TO DOS

MEALS TO NOURISH

GIVING & PREPARING

KEEPING HOME

A C T I O

KINDNESS TO MYSELF

How did I progress in living the Word today?

Tuesday, December 12
ROOTS & BRANCHES

Amos

A shepherd in Judah and the "dresser of sycamore trees," Amos was not a prophet by training; he didn't seek a job in prophecy. He was called to the extraordinary vocation by God. He has the distinction of being the first prophet to teach that a faithful remnant would survive a large-scale devastation. God called him at a time when Judah and Israel were living large—luxury and idleness ruled the people and the people of God were being corrupted by wealth and injustice. Amos sounded the alarm and tried to wake the complacent people to the perils of violating moral law. Amos spoke the truth of divine mercy and he extended to the Israelites the promise that God would return favor to the chosen people.

AMOS 9:11-12

On that day I will raise up
   the booth of David that is fallen,
and repair its breaches,
   and raise up its ruins,
   and rebuild it as in the days of old;
 in order that they may possess the remnant of Edom
   and all the nations who are called by my name,
   says the Lord who does this.

Acts 15:16-18
'After this I will return,
and I will rebuild the dwelling of David, which has fallen;
   from its ruins I will rebuild it,
      and I will set it up,
so that all other peoples may seek the Lord—
   even all the Gentiles over whom my name has been
called.
      Thus says the Lord, who has been making these
things known from long ago.'

FOR FURTHER READING

AMOS 3:12

AMOS 8:9

AMOS 9:8

MATTHEW 27:45

I always wanted to have a lot of children, but with two children under two, I found myself in a state of shock at how htard things were. My body was not my own, my time was not my own, and since I had never lost my baby weight the first time around, I was uncomfortably overweight, and feeling totally overwhelmed and unhealthy.

I decided to reclaim my life for myself. I got out all my old NFP charts, contacted an instructor who could help me chart while breastfeeding, and utterly and completely committed myself to having a solid chunk of time where my body was my own again. With disciplined dieting and working out, I lost 40 pounds in less than five months.

And, gradually, I stopped praying.

I wanted my life to be exclusively mine again. I had my plans and goals, and in my mind God had nothing to do with the decision to be open to more children. When our second baby was a little over one year old we discovered we had conceived, which was not my plan. I accepted it, but on the condition that things would still be mine—my body, my time, my life. I mentally resolved to not let this pregnancy change or affect the ways things were. My heart was hardened because I had stopped talking to God.

Then we lost our baby to miscarriage.

The darkness that surrounded me those first days of discovering our baby was no no longer living was thick, like a dense fog. So little hope was present there. I felt so much guilt over my selfishness and how much I had distanced myself from Our Lord. I knew that losing our baby was not punishment for my selfishness, but I experienced deep regret at my refusal to rejoice over that gift that God had given me, and at my decision to prize my vanity and desire for control over openness to new life.

Yet it was during those dark and difficult days that God moved in my heart, opening it to the gift of new life, and the gift of His life of grace working in me—more than almost any other time in my life. I grieved intensely at the loss of our baby, but I spoke to Our Lord intimately for the first time in a long time, and I invited Him back into my heart and my life in a new way. I began to gain new hope in His promises.

A new desire to give of myself for whatever children God wanted to give us welled up in my heart, and within a month or so of miscarrying, while my heart was still grieving and my body was still healing, we conceived again. The joy that followed the discovery of that pregnancy is one I can't describe.

Through Amos, God says that He will
> repair its breaches,
> and raise up its ruins,
> and rebuild it as in the days of old;

In Acts, too: I will rebuild the dwelling of David, which has fallen;
> from its ruins I will rebuild it,

Even in the midst of the waiting, He is working. He is restoring and healing and rebuilding, sometimes most especially when we can't see it or feel it.

As Christ was dying for us on the cross, the earth was darkened, but even in that darkness, hearts were being transformed, conversions were happening. The work Our Lord is doing in the midst of darkness can sometimes only be seen after the dawn, in the light of His resurrection.

In the darkness, God rebuilds the broken parts of our hearts; in the midst of death and grief, He can bring about new life. Amos speaks of the darkness which is a result of the sin of the Israelites, but he also prophesies a restoration in and through the coming Messiah, and in that prophecy there is hope, the hope of the newborn Babe.

ANA HAHN

Come Holy Spirit, fill the hearts of your faithful
and kindle in them the fire of your love.
Send forth your Spirit and they shall be created.
And You shall renew the face of the earth.
O, God, who by the light of the Holy Spirit,
did instruct the hearts of the faithful,
grant that by the same Holy Spirit we may be truly wise
and ever enjoy His consolations, Through Christ Our Lord,
Amen.

LECTIO

What is the objective meaning of the text?

Who do I encounter here and what do they say?

What is the how, the where, the when & the why?

MEDITATIO

What does the biblical text say to me?

What personal message does the text have for me?

What effect does the text have on my life?

ORATIO

What do I say to the Lord in response to His word?

What does the Lord want for me? How do I ask for grace? What is my song of of thanks for His gifts & praise for His glory?

CONTEMPLATIO

How does God see and judge reality? What conversion of mind, heart, and life is He asking of me today?

How has He conveyed His love for me in today's scripture?

Where is the beauty of His gifts and the goodness of His mercy?

How will I make my life a gift for others in charity?
What does God want me to do today?

TASKS & TO DOS

MEALS TO NOURISH

GIVING & PREPARING

KEEPING HOME

KINDNESS TO MYSELF

ACTIO

How did I progress in living the Word today?

Wednesday, December 13
ROOTS & BRANCHES

Micah

The prophet Micah was a contemporary of the prophets Isaiah, Amos, and Hosea. He lived when Samaria was the capital of the northern kingdom, Israel, and Jerusalem was the capital of the southern kingdom, Judah. Jeremiah tells us that Micah feared the Lord and sought His favor and repented before Him. Micah was gravely concerned about the moral and spiritual life of Judah. His book takes us back and forth between threats of doom and glimpses of glory. He offers us the realistic look at the hard plight of his people, and then he shares the great promise of the Messiah who will come from Bethlehem, the house of bread. From a humble stable beginning will rise a glorious King, who will allow Himself to enter under our roofs as the very Bread of Life.

MICAH 5:2-4

But you, O Bethlehem of Ephrathah,
    who are one of the little clans of Judah,
from you shall come forth for me
    one who is to rule in Israel,
whose origin is from of old,
    from ancient days.
Therefore he shall give them up until the time
    when she who is in labor has brought forth;
then the rest of his kindred shall return
    to the people of Israel.
And he shall stand and feed his flock in the strength of
the Lord,
    in the majesty of the name of the Lord his God.
And they shall live secure, for now he shall be great
    to the ends of the earth;

MICAH 7:20

You will show faithfulness to Jacob
    and unswerving loyalty to Abraham,
as you have sworn to our ancestors
    from the days of old.

FOR FURTHER READING

PSALMS 25:8-9

1 CORINTHIANS 10:31

I couldn't breathe.

I stood in the back of a church, too angry to approach the altar. The tabernacle's doors were closed tight and locked, just like my heart. I'd just come from seeing the doctor who'd shared his diagnosis of our son, Jonathan.

Jonathan was supposed to be the "normal" one. The one who didn't have extraordinary challenges. He wasn't supposed to struggle with depression and PTSD. He wasn't supposed to drop out of college, come home, and turn into an angry Hulk. Jonathan was my baby boy, my wonder kid, my pride and joy.

But that day, the doctor explained my son's deep trauma. After years of watching his sister experience seizure after seizure, waiting for her to start breathing again, and therefore never experiencing a typical life, Jonathan suffered from "survivor's guilt." He was in pain and needed professional help.

There was nothing I could do. My heart was broken. And I believed it was God's fault.

God had betrayed me again. He'd allowed my daughter to suffer. Now my son wanted to give up on life because of the pain--pain that God could stop at any moment but chose not to.

I stared at the tabernacle and wanted to hurl things. There was no room in my heart for Jesus. No room for anything but anger and disappointment. As the tears fell, I silently screamed at God. When I was done, I left the church feeling no peace. I promised myself I'd never return.

For the next few days, my husband and I listened as Jonathan poured out his hurt.

"You love Courtney more than me."
"It's not fair that Courtney suffers when I'm fine."

"It should be me. I'm stronger than Courtney. I can take it."

Our hearts grew heavier every day that passed. My anger had not abated.

At my husband's request, I returned to church the next Sunday. Once seated in the pew, knowing I was still angry, Jerry whispered, "It's not God's fault. Everything is going to be OK. He's walked us through the valley with Courtney. He won't abandon Jonathan."

My husband didn't know what he was asking me to do. I didn't hear the readings or the Gospel. I'd begun an internal dialogue with God that was more rant than conversation. Forget the praise and worship!

During Consecration, Courtney laughed when the bells rang as she always did. But that day it took me by surprise. Jonathan whispered, "Courtney knows Jesus is here. She knows it better than we do." He held her hand as the priest lifted Our Lord above the altar.

I stared at the Host, now transformed into the Body of Christ, and my heart hurt. I fought desperately to hang on to those feelings of discontent. I looked at my children. Jonathan still believed Jesus was present and he was the one in distress. Courtney believed because she knew only love.

I fought hard to hold onto my pain, I'd turned Jesus away just like the innkeeper turned away Joseph and Mary. I told myself there was no room for God. No room for Jesus. No room for the Holy Spirit. The fact that I was surprised when Courtney laughed during the Consecration proves how little room there was in my heart.

Despite the "No Vacancy" sign I put up, God kept knocking. As I waited in the Communion line, taking one small step after another, it dawned on me that, in the Eucharist, we receive our Lord, but only if we open our hearts to Him.

At first, I resented His persistence because I'm stubborn. I like to be right. But as I waited to receive our Lord, my heart opened like the Tabernacle doors, and the ache in my shoulders lessened. My fists unclenched, and my breath evened out.

God was asking for a place to dwell, and despite my lingering doubt, I took the "No Vacancy" sign down. It would take months to work toward complete peace with what was happening with my son. But after receiving Communion that day, I offered God a resting place that, while not the Ritz, was all for Him. In this Advent season, God is not looking for the Ritz; He is just looking to reside in the humble stable of your heart, with its messiness, broken pieces, and dark corners. Are you willing to make room and allow Him in?

MARY LENABURG

HE IS JUST LOOKING
TO RESIDE IN THE HUMBLE
STABLE OF YOUR HEART,
WITH ITS MESSINESS,
BROKEN PIECES,
AND DARK CORNERS.

MARY LENABURG

Come Holy Spirit, fill the hearts of your faithful
and kindle in them the fire of your love.
Send forth your Spirit and they shall be created.
And You shall renew the face of the earth.
O, God, who by the light of the Holy Spirit,
did instruct the hearts of the faithful,
grant that by the same Holy Spirit we may be truly wise
and ever enjoy His consolations, Through Christ Our Lord,
Amen.

LECTIO

What is the objective meaning of the text?

Who do I encounter here and what do they say?

What is the how, the where, the when & the why?

MEDITATIO

What does the biblical text say to me?

What personal message does the text have for me?

What effect does the text have on my life?

ORATIO

What do I say to the Lord in response to His word?

What does the Lord want for me? How do I ask for grace? What is my song of of thanks for His gifts & praise for His glory?

CONTEMPLATIO

How does God see and judge reality? What conversion of mind, heart, and life is He asking of me today?

How has He conveyed His love for me in today's scripture?

Where is the beauty of His gifts and the goodness of His mercy?

How will I make my life a gift for others in charity?
What does God want me to do today?

TASKS & TO DOS

MEALS TO NOURISH

GIVING & PREPARING

ACTIO

KEEPING HOME

KINDNESS TO MYSELF

How did I progress in living the Word today?

Thursday, December 14
ROOTS & BRANCHES

Jonah

Jonah's notorious saga began with disobedience. He really didn't want to be a prophet, and rather than obeying right away, he became a sterling example of both the consequences of delayed obedience and the divine mercy God so wants to extend. God called Jonah to go to Ninevah and call the people there to repentance. But Jonah, overcome by his hatred of the foreign land and its people, fled by sea in the other direction. A storm arose and the sailors in the boat with Jonah agreed that the storm was a curse. When they drew lots to see who was the source of the curse, Jonah confessed his disobedience and was thrown overboard. A giant fish swallowed him—God's providence against drowning. Jonah called out to God for mercy and mercy was extended; after three days, the fish vomited him onto land. This time, Jonah went to Nineveh and warned the people of impending doom. To his astonishment, they listened to him and amended their ways. Jonah's time in the dark, dank belly of the fish, from which he emerged miraculously incorrupt, foreshadowed Jesus' time in the dark, dank tomb, from which he emerged into the light, defeating death and opening the gates of paradise.

But the story doesn't end there, and our Scripture study today takes us to Jonah's stubborn persistence in hatred of Ninevah and the way his greediness and racism threatens to consume him.

JONAH 4: 6-11

The Lord God appointed a bush, and made it come up over Jonah, to give shade over his head, to save him from his discomfort; so Jonah was very happy about the bush. But when dawn came up the next day, God appointed a worm that attacked the bush, so that it withered. When the sun rose, God prepared a sultry east wind, and the sun beat down on the head of Jonah so that he was faint and asked that he might die. He said, "It is better for me to die than to live." But God said to Jonah, "Is it right for you to be angry about the bush?" And he said, "Yes, angry enough to die." Then the Lord said, "You are concerned about the bush, for which you did not labor and which you did not grow; it came into being in a night and perished in a night. And should I not be concerned about Nineveh, that great city, in which there are more than a hundred and twenty thousand persons who do not know their right hand from their left, and also many animals?"

FOR FURTHER READING

READ THE BOOK OF JONAH

(IT'S NOT THAT LONG!)

Jonah is a tale for our times. A racist, nationalistic, supremacist who is stingy with God's message, he's the perfect prophet for this year. Jonah, an Assyrian chief, was asked by God to go to Nineveh, a Gentile city, and warn the people to amend their ways. But he didn't go. Instead, he went off in a different direction across the Mediterranean Sea. When he was thrown overboard, God saved him from drowning by providing a great fish to swallow him and then to regurgitate him three days later.

Jonah is an Easter story, to be sure. Three days in the tomb of the giant fish, and then a second chance at life foretells Jesus' burial and resurrection. But it's also an Advent story, because Advent is about preparing for the birth of Mercy Incarnate. Jesus came to save the world, to teach us how to have good will toward our enemies. Jesus came to show us how to bless the people who curse us. He came to extend mercy to the world. Jonah does not want to be an instrument in the repentance of Nineveh and the restoration of that land to God. He wants God to smite them. Following his time in the tomb of the great fish, he reconsiders and obeys God's call, but he's still not persuaded by mercy.

After Jonah's infamous stay in the belly of the fish, after he goes to Nineveh and the people listen to him, after God has poured out patient mercy on Jonah, he's still a racist. He wanted the people of Nineveh to perish, and he's mad that God was rich in love and ready to turn punishment into forgiveness. God provides a bush to give Jonah shade from the Mediterranean sun, and the prophet sits sulking in the shade. Then, in a brilliant stroke of excellent lesson planning, God provides a worm to kill his shade plant, and then wind and heat are employed to make him more uncomfortable. Sometimes, God's provision feels like the nasty belly of a fish. Sometimes, it's the heat and wind of a scorching day. Sometimes God's mercy does not feel tender at all. Instead, it's a miserable existence that might just make us turn to God and repent. God has saved Nineveh. But will Jonah allow Him to save Jonah?

As the sun beats down on Jonah's head, he feels faint and begs to die. He is so angry over the salvation of Nineveh that he tells the Lord that he is being consumed by the heat of his hate. That's some pretty serious racism. God speaks into that hate, and points out that Jonah neither planted nor watered the shade tree; he had no provision over it. God tells him that Nineveh, by contrast, was full of people about whom God cared deeply and for whom He wanted restoration.

God loves to show mercy. And God loves for us to love mercy. There are no ethnic barriers to God's love, and so, there should be no ethnic barriers to ours, either. Like Jonah, like Nineveh, like the plant, we owe our lives to God.

With that life, you are called to do justice, to love mercy, and to act humbly with our God (Micah 6:8).

That means that Christmas is not just for the people you gather around your table, or just about the people with whom you gather in your church. To truly celebrate this season, you have to embrace people outside your circle. You have to open the doors of that stable to Christians who worship in ways different than you do, whose doctrine is not precisely what yours is. And you have to impart the love of the Infant to people who don't know Him at all.

You are His hands and feet here on this earth. He wants you to go to Nineveh. Maybe you got sidetracked. Maybe your life right now feels as uncomfortable as the inside of a giant fish. Maybe the wind is blowing hot and dusty in your face. Maybe you need to stop thinking about yourself and your quirks and your prejudicial idiosyncrasies and pour out that energy in love on someone different from you. Maybe, today's the day to do that.

ELIZABETH FOSS

Come Holy Spirit, fill the hearts of your faithful
and kindle in them the fire of your love.
Send forth your Spirit and they shall be created.
And You shall renew the face of the earth.
O, God, who by the light of the Holy Spirit,
did instruct the hearts of the faithful,
grant that by the same Holy Spirit we may be truly wise
and ever enjoy His consolations, Through Christ Our Lord,
Amen.

LECTIO

What is the objective meaning of the text?

Who do I encounter here and what do they say?

What is the how, the where, the when & the why?

MEDITATIO

What does the biblical text say to me?

What personal message does the text have for me?

What effect does the text have on my life?

ORATIO

What do I say to the Lord in response to His word?

What does the Lord want for me? How do I ask for grace? What is my song of of thanks for His gifts & praise for His glory?

CONTEMPLATIO

How does God see and judge reality? What conversion of mind, heart, and life is He asking of me today?

How has He conveyed His love for me in today's scripture?

Where is the beauty of His gifts and the goodness of His mercy?

How will I make my life a gift for others in charity?
What does God want me to do today?

TASKS & TO DOS

MEALS TO NOURISH

GIVING & PREPARING

KEEPING HOME

KINDNESS TO MYSELF

ACTIO

How did I progress in living the Word today?

Friday, December 15
ROOTS & BRANCHES

Habakkuk

Habakkuk, whose name means "loving embrace," lived
during a time of wickedness and warned his people of
the Chaldean invasion of Judah. He offers a warning for
us, too, asking us how we will live in order to bring life
and not death at the time of judgment. Can we hear the
prophet's voice now, as we ready to turn the calendar
page to a new year in times that are also very uncertain?
"The just shall live by his faith" (2:4). Even if times
are trying, can we, like Habakkuk, rejoice in the Lord?
Habakkuk didn't know how God would both hate sin
and save the sinner, but God revealed to him that it was
so, and Habakkuk stepped out in faith to proclaim it. As
we continue our journey towards Christmas, we have the
tender mercy of knowing that it was Christ who will be
born to show eternal mercy on sinners.

HABAKKUK 2:1-4

I will stand at my watchpost,
    and station myself on the rampart;
I will keep watch to see what he will say to me,
    and what he will answer concerning my complaint.
 Then the Lord answered me and said:
Write the vision;
    make it plain on tablets,
    so that a runner may read it.
For there is still a vision for the appointed time;
    it speaks of the end, and does not lie.
If it seems to tarry, wait for it;
    it will surely come, it will not delay.
Look at the proud!
    Their spirit is not right in them,
    but the righteous live by their faith

HABAKKUK 3:2

O Lord, I have heard of your renown,
    and I stand in awe, O Lord, of your work.
In our own time revive it;
    in our own time make it known;
    in wrath may you remember mercy.

HABAKKUK 3:16-19

I hear, and I tremble within;
    my lips quiver at the sound.
Rottenness enters into my bones,
    and my steps tremble beneath me.
I wait quietly for the day of calamity
    to come upon the people who attack us.

Though the fig tree does not blossom,
    and no fruit is on the vines;
though the produce of the olive fails,
    and the fields yield no food;
though the flock is cut off from the fold,
    and there is no herd in the stalls,
yet I will rejoice in the Lord;
    I will exult in the God of my salvation.
God, the Lord, is my strength;
    he makes my feet like the feet of a deer,
    and makes me tread upon the heights.

TAKE UP & READ

It doesn't take more than a minute of the news to hear that our world is filled with struggle, pain, and suffering. It seems that as soon as one conflict is resolved, there's one to take its place. And even in my personal life—while I'm so thankful for the storms that have passed—I stumble under the weight of what seems like one new storm after another. There are conflicts and problems I can't solve, and many days, it's hard to trust that resolution will ever come.

Habakkuk also lived in times of great conflict. He too felt the weight of struggle and suffering. He didn't have answers to the problems of his time, nor could he understand why God didn't just stop those doing evil. And when he asked, "Why?" he got a difficult response: wait. God revealed plans for the righteous to triumph over the evil—plans that seemed almost unbelievable to Habakkuk—but told Habakkuk he must wait, and in the meantime, live by his faith. Habakkuk questioned God's plan, but eventually embraced a life of faith, choosing to trust and even rejoice in God's promises. And God did indeed fulfill them, working in incredible ways to end the evil of Habakkuk's time.

When I cry out to God in frustration, I often hear Him say that I need to wait, too. This is the point at which I used to give up in the past.

Years ago, I was in a very unhealthy relationship. A person I trusted took advantage of my naivety, leaving me hurt and confused. I couldn't find a way out, and didn't think I ever would. I prayed more fervently than I ever had before, but God didn't answer my prayer in the way I expected or wanted. The hurt continued for a long time, until I finally found the strength to walk away. Even then, the person who'd hurt me expressed no remorse. It didn't seem like God had heard my pleas, and in my frustration, I hardened my heart and stopped praying—stopped believing He was even there at all.

Thankfully, beyond my wildest dreams, I found my way back to God several years later. During that time, there were two practices that strengthened my faith and taught me to live in hopefulness—to rest in Him and wait for redemption—even when it looks like evil has won. Habakkuk used these practices, too.

The first is dialogue. Instead of shutting down and hardening his heart, Habakkuk kept talking. God can take our hard questions, and wants them, even when they come from a place of anger or frustration. Because when we're asking questions, we're still engaging. It's when we shut down and turn away that our faith is most at most risk of wavering.

The second practice is reflection. Habakkuk recounted the history of his people and in doing so, recognized how God worked in the past. Reflecting on our own past trials often allows God's presence to become clear in a way it wasn't at the time. And when we begin to see God's hand in the difficult periods of our lives, our faith is strengthened, fortifying us for struggles we will inevitably face in the future. Reflecting on those spiritually dark years in my past, I see now that God was making a way for me to move towards healing and greater self-confidence through the love of others in my life. Evil did not win, love did.

I still wait to see how God will redeem many conflicts and problems in our world and in my life. The waiting is not easy. But it's easier when I embrace a life of faith like Habakkuk, keeping dialogue with God open, and looking for His hand in the past.

Jesus told us that He has overcome the world, and that He is the way to peace. When we trust this, and live by our faith—even in our waiting—we can share that gift with others, bringing greater peace to the kingdom on earth while we keep our eyes fixed on the kingdom of heaven.

ALLISON MCGINLEY

Come Holy Spirit, fill the hearts of your faithful
and kindle in them the fire of your love.
Send forth your Spirit and they shall be created.
And You shall renew the face of the earth.
O, God, who by the light of the Holy Spirit,
did instruct the hearts of the faithful,
grant that by the same Holy Spirit we may be truly wise
and ever enjoy His consolations, Through Christ Our Lord,
Amen.

LECTIO

What is the objective meaning of the text?

Who do I encounter here and what do they say?

What is the how, the where, the when & the why?

MEDITATIO

What does the biblical text say to me?

What personal message does the text have for me?

What effect does the text have on my life?

ORATIO

What do I say to the Lord in response to His word?

What does the Lord want for me? How do I ask for grace? What is my song of of thanks for His gifts & praise for His glory?

CONTEMPLATIO

How does God see and judge reality? What conversion of mind, heart, and life is He asking of me today?

How has He conveyed His love for me in today's scripture?

Where is the beauty of His gifts and the goodness of His mercy?

LECTIO DIVINA | DECEMBER 15

How will I make my life a gift for others in charity?
What does God want me to do today?

TASKS & TO DOS

MEALS TO NOURISH

GIVING & PREPARING

ACTIO

KEEPING HOME

KINDNESS TO MYSELF

How did I progress in living the Word today?

Saturday, December 16
SCRIPTURE MEMORY

Memorizing Scripture makes it our own. When we commit it to our hearts, we always have it to carry wherever we go. This week, remember that the Lord will strengthen you to the end. It's a journey, and He's taking it with you. This week, we repeat with Mary the words of the Magnificat. Let us be fully aware of the great things He has done for us, and let us continue to glorify His name.

Today is a day to rest and be grateful. Take some time to look over your journaling from the week, to read a little more, to catch up on days when you didn't have as much time as you would have liked.
Spend a few moments looking carefully at our memory verses, to burn the image into your brain. Then write them yourself on the weekly planning page and read them again and again when you refer to the tasks of the your weekly to-dos.

One more thing: if there is a child in your life, teach these words to him or her and don't be surprised when the child memorizes more easily than you do, even when the verses are longer! This memory work is a gift, a legacy. Hiding the Word of God in the heart of child is stocking his soul with saving grace. Together, take on this joyful endeavor. We're right there with you.

Luke 1:49-50

"For He who is mighty has done great things for me, and holy is His Name. And His mercy is on those who fear Him from generation to generation."

Holy is His Name

LUKE 1:49-50

Third Week of Advent

Week of Sunday, December 17

SUNDAY | DECEMBER 17

MONDAY | DECEMBER 18

TUESDAY | NDECEMBER 19

WEDNESDAY | DECEMBER 20

THURSDAY | DECEMBER 21

FRIDAY | DECEMBER 22

SATURDAY | DECEMBER 23

feast day celebration ideas

Third Week of Advent

memory verse

give + prepare

PSALM 36: 7-9

prayer requests

Sunday, December 17
THIRD SUNDAY OF ADVENT

1 THESSALONIANS 5:16-24

Rejoice always, pray without ceasing, give thanks in all circumstances; for this is the will of God in Christ Jesus for you. Do not quench the Spirit. Do not despise the words of prophets, but test everything; hold fast to what is good; abstain from every form of evil. May the God of peace himself sanctify you entirely; and may your spirit and soul and body be kept sound and blameless at the coming of our Lord Jesus Christ. The one who calls you is faithful, and he will do this.

FOR FURTHER READING

JOHN 1:6-8, 19-28

ISAIAH 61:1-2A, 10-11

There are days that begin with tall orders. Days that are bursting with opportunity to do the work of mercy. Days when you hear the Lord saying that He appeals to you as his daughter "to respect those who labor among you, and have charge of you in the Lord and admonish you; esteem them very highly in love because of their work. Be at peace among yourselves." Further, He urges you "to admonish the idlers, encourage the fainthearted, help the weak, be patient with all of them. See that none of you repays evil for evil, but always seek to do good to one another and to all" (see 1 Thessalonians 5:12-15).

Oh. That's all? How in the world does one live up to that charge? By listening just a little longer and hearing God's plan for living a life of holy service. Those verses are followed by the ones in the second reading today. Saint Paul tells us to rejoice always and to pray without ceasing. The two go together.

If we were to try to rejoice always, in all circumstances, we'd fail miserably. It is not humanly possible to rejoice about everything that happens or doesn't happen. But we aren't called to rejoice in the gritty, difficult details of life; we are called to rejoice in God and His promise to be with us when people disappoint us and life gets hard. We draw from His goodness to daily to meet the challenges of the day and rejoice in whatever they hold for us. Saint Paul anticipates the next obvious question.

How do we rejoice? How do we keep God's promises front and center so that we remember that He's there in the messes and we can rest in that? We pray without ceasing and we give thanks in everything. This is the life-giving sequence of thought that needs to crowd out the the thoughts of self-doubt or anger or frustration. If we are able to keep an inner dialogue of prayer going, and if were are mindful of every tender mercy and give thanks for it, we can live lives that are spiritually fruitful regardless of what befalls us.

God tells us how to pray. He tells us how to stay in His presence and go about our days, living out our lives as prayers in action. Saint Paul calls us to holy behavior, then he reminds us that God makes us holy. It is Christ who sanctifies us. He uses our prayers to sanctify, seamlessly weaving a lifestyle of sanctity into a holy life.

There are moments, days, even whole seasons when we don't feel like we're making any progress at all in the spiritual life. God assures us that He is still at work during those dry times. We worry that He tells us to retain only what is good and to refrain from every kind of evil, and we fail at that over and over again. How can we possibly be progressing towards holiness? Read on, my friend. Read on.

We don't make ourselves holy. God makes us holy. He calls us into the pursuit of holiness and then He alone perfects us (v. 23,24). Today, what He wants is for us to trust Him. He humbled Himself to be born into this life in order to forgive our sins. We believe that. We celebrate that, beginning with Christmas and culminating in Easter. If He can forgive our sins, He can also supply the grace as necessary to become perfectly holy and entirely blameless—to progress in this lifetime, little by little, as His grace makes us more and more like Jesus.

God is faithful, and He will finish His good work in you. Of this, you can be assured.

ELIZABETH FOSS

Come Holy Spirit, fill the hearts of your faithful
and kindle in them the fire of your love.
Send forth your Spirit and they shall be created.
And You shall renew the face of the earth.
O, God, who by the light of the Holy Spirit,
did instruct the hearts of the faithful,
grant that by the same Holy Spirit we may be truly wise
and ever enjoy His consolations, Through Christ Our Lord,
Amen.

LECTIO

What is the objective meaning of the text?

Who do I encounter here and what do they say?

What is the how, the where, the when & the why?

MEDITATIO

What does the biblical text say to me?

What personal message does the text have for me?

What effect does the text have on my life?

ORATIO

What do I say to the Lord in response to His word?

What does the Lord want for me? How do I ask for grace? What is my song of of thanks for His gifts & praise for His glory?

CONTEMPLATIO

How does God see and judge reality? What conversion of mind, heart, and life is He asking of me today?

How has He conveyed His love for me in today's scripture?

Where is the beauty of His gifts and the goodness of His mercy?

How will I make my life a gift for others in charity?
What does God want me to do today?

TASKS & TO DOS

MEALS TO NOURISH

GIVING & PREPARING

KEEPING HOME

ACTIO

KINDNESS TO MYSELF

How did I progress in living the Word today?

Monday, December 18
ROOTS & BRANCHES

Isaiah

Prophet and poet, Isaiah's deep love and devotion to the Lord resonates throughout his writing. He was a prophet with a difficult mission during a difficult time. He was to tell of the fall of Israel and the chastisement of Judah, but his words fell on the ears of people enjoying peace and plenty. As the hard times came to be, he was a comforter and consoler. Of all the prophets, it was Isaiah who gave us the richest, clearest Old Testament vision of the Messiah. With Jerusalem under siege and the future looking anything but certain, the poet-prophet issued forth beautiful Immanuel prophecies in brilliant literary style. His spiritual insights were so enduring and so profoundly expressed that Isaiah is the prophet who is most often quoted in the New Testament.

ISAIAH 41:9-10

you whom I took from the ends of the earth,
  and called from its farthest corners,
saying to you, "You are my servant,
  I have chosen you and not cast you off";
 do not fear, for I am with you,
  do not be afraid, for I am your God;
I will strengthen you, I will help you,
  I will uphold you with my victorious right hand.

ISAIAH 54:10-11

For the mountains may depart
  and the hills be removed,
but my steadfast love shall not depart from you,
  and my covenant of peace shall not be removed,
  says the Lord, who has compassion on you.
O afflicted one, storm-tossed, and not comforted,
  I am about to set your stones in antimony,
  and lay your foundations with sapphires.

FOR FURTHER READING

GALATIANS 2:20

PROVERBS 3:5-6

This is not where I planned to write tonight. The dining room walls are a familiar shade of cranberry. My brothers are in the next room over, finishing up summer assignments for their first week of school. My parents are asleep upstairs. My little sister is tucked away in her new home in a southern town.

I did not plan to be back in my childhood home this late in the season, on the hem of September. In fact, I should be writing tonight from a place very far from here, from an old house in rural England. My intended flight took off without me last night. My new departure date is elusive.

A delayed visa application has set back my plans. It's pushed back my start date for a teaching fellowship I'm anxious to begin. It's cut into the time that I want there to settle into a new town, a new country, a new community.

I'm not a planner. I prefer to let events unfold as they may. I am a firm believer that things happen for a reason, and who am I to question? But every once in awhile, I eat my words. Often in the face of change, when I am scared the rug is going to be ripped out from under me, I stare at the rising tide of uncertainty and scramble for control.

All summer, I've dreaded the unknown, the changes that were sure to come at me quicker than I could prepare. So I planned. I planned and I planned until I was sure nothing could knock me down this round. I'm entering a time of transition. My friends have all found new corners of the universe to inhabit. I left my beautiful, though broken, Charlottesville right on the cusp of tragedy. As my little sister settles into her first year of college, my family will once again recalibrate their operations at home, just as they did when I left for school.

And I've found myself in the middle of it all. Not fully here, but not yet gone. Frustrated that I wasn't on that flight last night. Frustrated that I'm not able to start the next chapter. Frustrated that my plan, my calculated and vainly crafted plan, has been washed away. It's a sheet with running ink.

Sometimes my plan is not His plan. And His plan is always better.

God kept me here longer than I intended, but He has already shown me why in abundance. He's given me time to throw all of my energy into Take Up & Read. He's granted me the opportunity to spend time with my family before I leave them for ten months. He's caused me to pause, to open my heart to the alternative, to the unconventional path.

Yes, this week hasn't gone according to plan. But it means that I am here, nestled in my Virginia home for a little while longer. I am here and it is my choice how fully I want to be here, how present I choose to be. I can keep one foot out the door, or I can spend these last few weeks stateside fully opening up my heart to the presence of the One who will see me through it.

I can invite Him in. I can spend time with my Bible open at this familiar dining room table. I can spend my afternoons in the parish where I received my first sacraments. I can firmly root myself in the familiar, so that I am ready when it is time to leave. Ready to face the uncertainty. Ready to carry out His word and mission in a new place. Ready to answer the call I don't see coming.

CARLY BUCKHOLZ

Come Holy Spirit, fill the hearts of your faithful
and kindle in them the fire of your love.
Send forth your Spirit and they shall be created.
And You shall renew the face of the earth.
O, God, who by the light of the Holy Spirit,
did instruct the hearts of the faithful,
grant that by the same Holy Spirit we may be truly wise
and ever enjoy His consolations, Through Christ Our Lord,
Amen.

LECTIO

What is the objective meaning of the text?

Who do I encounter here and what do they say?

What is the how, the where, the when & the why?

MEDITATIO

What does the biblical text say to me?

What personal message does the text have for me?

What effect does the text have on my life?

ORATIO

What do I say to the Lord in response to His word?

What does the Lord want for me? How do I ask for grace? What is my song of of thanks for His gifts & praise for His glory?

CONTEMPLATIO

How does God see and judge reality? What conversion of mind, heart, and life is He asking of me today?

How has He conveyed His love for me in today's scripture?

Where is the beauty of His gifts and the goodness of His mercy?

How will I make my life a gift for others in charity?
What does God want me to do today?

TASKS & TO DOS

MEALS TO NOURISH

GIVING & PREPARING

ACTIO

KEEPING HOME

KINDNESS TO MYSELF

How did I progress in living the Word today?

Tuesday, December 19
ROOTS & BRANCHES

Jeremiah

Jeremiah is sometimes called the weeping prophet because he wept bitterly for the sins of his people. During the time of Jeremiah, God's chosen ones lived captive in a foreign land. Through the tears of His prophet, God offered hope—that a righteous Branch, a great King, would one day reign in the hearts of the faithful. God spoke this hope to Jeremiah as he watched a potter work wet clay on a wheel. As he was working, the vessel—the one he'd so carefully crafted—fell apart, right in his hands. Instead of giving up and abandoning his wheel, he took the ruined lump of clay and created something new. Watching the potter work his craft, Jeremiah knew that God had revealed something about Himself—that He takes what is broken and makes it whole. Jeremiah's story offers us the hope that God would take a fallen people, broken vessels, and make them new. He took a simple man named Jesse, the humble stump, and from him grew a many-branched tree. And from the growth of Jesse's tree, God formed a new vessel—the womb of a Virgin. The Divine Potter not only crafted it, but also made His dwelling in it. He took on the flesh of the Virgin, yours and mine, and recreated us.

JEREMIAH 18:1-11

The word that came to Jeremiah from the Lord: "Come, go down to the potter's house, and there I will let you hear my words." So I went down to the potter's house, and there he was working at his wheel. The vessel he was making of clay was spoiled in the potter's hand, and he reworked it into another vessel, as seemed good to him. Then the word of the Lord came to me: Can I not do with you, O house of Israel, just as this potter has done? says the Lord. Just like the clay in the potter's hand, so are you in my hand, O house of Israel. At one moment I may declare concerning a nation or a kingdom, that I will pluck up and break down and destroy it, but if that nation, concerning which I have spoken, turns from its evil, I will change my mind about the disaster that I intended to bring on it. And at another moment I may declare concerning a nation or a kingdom that I will build and plant it, but if it does evil in my sight, not listening to my voice, then I will change my mind about the good that I had intended to do to it. Now, therefore, say to the people of Judah and the inhabitants of Jerusalem: Thus says the Lord: Look, I am a potter shaping evil against you and devising a plan against you. Turn now, all of you from your evil way, and amend your ways and your doings.

FOR FURTHER READING

2 TIMOTHY 1: 6-8

ISAIAH 64:8

ROMANS 9:20-21

With six kids in the house, I can predict the breaking of an item with alarming accuracy. When it comes to predicting the brokenness of my own spirituality? That one blind-sided me.

In the spring of 2009, I was the perfect mom. Yes, child number two had been a handful of a baby, but nothing a boppy, a tight swaddle, and earplugs for mom couldn't fix. My four children kept me busy, but with one in school and three at home, I had hit my parenting stride. My fridge was stocked with Dr Pepper and I was well on my way to becoming the Catholic Martha Stewart.

Then, I got pregnant with baby number five, Luke. At my 20-week ultrasound we learned I had a placental tumor and the baby wasn't growing well. The next few days, weeks, and months our lives were filled with perinatologist appointments, blood draws, ultrasounds and a boatload of worry, imaginary scenarios I dreamed up, and fear. Then came the unplanned C-section, the neonatal intensive care unit 44-day stay, the emergency surgery, and our son, coding and being resuscitated. I mean, what baby stops breathing while his parents are three floors up, praying with a priest?

Nothing breaks you open quite like hearing the doctor say, "We're going to do everything we can to save him."

If this is how the potter treats His clay, then I want no part of it. How, amidst God's great wisdom, could He use my child to break me open, to make me whole? How could the seven surgeries, the twelve specialists, the hundreds of therapy appointments, the thousands of hours we spent teaching our son to eat, and a marriage that found itself in counseling—how could those make me whole? With each one of those setbacks, I could feel a part of my soul being broken, normal bit by normal bit.

It was during Luke's seventh surgery where I found myself standing on the second floor outdoor balcony, adjacent to the hospital's tiny chapel. Luke was cradled in my arms and I was relishing in the quiet moment. The night was dark, just after dusk, and the breeze carried the smallest hint of humidity. Out there, nothing smelled like the antiseptic hospital behind us and I could see a few lit hospital windows here and there. It was then, I spotted it. The NICU is located on the fourth floor and I could see nurses, bustling around what looked to be a new inhabitant.

I caught my breath. Four years ago, I had stood in that same NICU, at roughly the same time of year, wondering if our son was going to live through the night. Oh, if only I could've shared with the Kathryn of yesteryear what the Kathryn of that moment knew.

She would survive and be whole once again.

Luke's middle name is Timothy, taken from the readings the weekend he was born:

"For this reason I remind you to rekindle the gift of God that is within you through the laying on of my hands, for God did not give us a spirit of cowardice, but rather a spirit of power and of love and of self-discipline. Do not be ashamed, then, of the testimony about our Lord or of me his prisoner, but join with me in suffering for the gospel, relying on the power of God." (2 Timothy 1: 6-8)

It was in my brokenness that I could finally strip away all the barriers I had put up to knowing and loving my Maker in a real and tangible way. The jealousy and the materialism, the pride and the righteousness—they were chipped away, my exterior broken, so that my interior could be made new. It hurt, y'all. It was painful to realize my shortcomings and my inadequate human self. But, dang, was it beautiful to see how God shaped me to love Him with the kind of love that is eternal. I found my purpose. For when you suffer big, you learn to lean in and love big.

You really are made whole.

And praise the sweet Lord for that.

KATHRYN WHITAKER

Come Holy Spirit, fill the hearts of your faithful
and kindle in them the fire of your love.
Send forth your Spirit and they shall be created.
And You shall renew the face of the earth.
O, God, who by the light of the Holy Spirit,
did instruct the hearts of the faithful,
grant that by the same Holy Spirit we may be truly wise
and ever enjoy His consolations, Through Christ Our Lord,
Amen.

LECTIO

What is the objective meaning of the text?

Who do I encounter here and what do they say?

What is the how, the where, the when & the why?

MEDITATIO

What does the biblical text say to me?

What personal message does the text have for me?

What effect does the text have on my life?

ORATIO

What do I say to the Lord in response to His word?

What does the Lord want for me? How do I ask for grace? What is my song of of thanks for His gifts & praise for His glory?

CONTEMPLATIO

How does God see and judge reality? What conversion of mind, heart, and life is He asking of me today?

How has He conveyed His love for me in today's scripture?

Where is the beauty of His gifts and the goodness of His mercy?

How will I make my life a gift for others in charity?
What does God want me to do today?

TASKS & TO DOS

MEALS TO NOURISH

GIVING & PREPARING

KEEPING HOME

ACTIO

KINDNESS TO MYSELF

How did I progress in living the Word today?

Wednesday, December 20
ROOTS & BRANCHES

Ezekiel

Ezekiel, whose name means "God will strengthen," was, indeed, a stalwart man of God. He lived in a community of Jewish exiles on a river in Babylonia. A man of strong will, who was distinguished by his firm character, he was respected by his community and his elders consulted him on all matters. A widower who lost his wife suddenly, he was notably devoted to his faith—to the rituals and rites of the Hebrews trained in the Levitical tradition. Ezekiel is thought to have been a cheerful man who embraced his calling as a prophet with a peacefulness of heart that enabled him to rise to its challenges with grace and good will. He ardently loved his people and he served them faithfully and well.

EZEKIEL 10:1-5

Then I looked, and above the dome that was over the heads of the cherubim there appeared above them something like a sapphire, in form resembling a throne. He said to the man clothed in linen, "Go within the wheelwork underneath the cherubim; fill your hands with burning coals from among the cherubim, and scatter them over the city." He went in as I looked on. Now the cherubim were standing on the south side of the house when the man went in; and a cloud filled the inner court. Then the glory of the Lord rose up from the cherub to the threshold of the house; the house was filled with the cloud, and the court was full of the brightness of the glory of the Lord. The sound of the wings of the cherubim was heard as far as the outer court, like the voice of God Almighty when he speaks.

EZEKIEL 10:18-19

Then the glory of the Lord went out from the threshold of the house and stopped above the cherubim. The cherubim lifted up their wings and rose up from the earth in my sight as they went out with the wheels beside them. They stopped at the entrance of the east gate of the house of the Lord; and the glory of the God of Israel was above them.

FOR FURTHER READING

EZEKIEL 1

EZEKIEL 44:1-3

JOHN 1:1-18

Ezekiel was a prophet in exile, far from his homeland. He lived as a stranger in a foreign land, a refugee in Babylon. In Ezekiel's lifetime, Nebuchadnezzar destroyed both Jerusalem and its Temple, the place where God's glory dwelt. For the Jews, to see the destruction of the Temple was to witness the loss of the presence of God among them. Nothing could have been more devastating.

While in exile, Ezekiel was given a vision of God's glorious throne—a vision of hope, one that promised that God's presence wasn't limited to the Jerusalem Temple. We know the fulfillment of this vision. It's what we're preparing to celebrate, that God is with us. According to Saint John's gospel, the true Temple of God is not a structure made of stone but a Body, one taken from a Virgin. To enter into this mystery is the purpose of Advent: to know and adore the real and everlasting Temple. This Temple was not one not made by human hands, but through the overshadowing of the Holy Spirit in the womb of the humble Virgin Mary. This season we prepare our hearts to enter into the eternal reality that God is with us. Emmanuel.

God made His dwelling among us. In his gospel, St. John writes that He literally tabernacled among us. Jesus was born in a city named Bethlehem, meaning House of Bread. And He remains with us, in the tabernacles of our churches as the Bread of Life. He was born in a place that spoke of food and He perpetually makes Himself our divine nourishment. He rests in the tabernacles of our hearts when we receive Him in the Eucharist. God is with us.

Like Ezekiel, we too are exiled in this life, living far away from our homeland—Heaven. But the thing about the life of grace is that right here, in this material world and in our physical bodies, we can experience a foretaste of our homeland. Like Ezekiel, we are strangers in a foreign land and our longing for God bears witness to that. But we aren't limited to visions as Ezekiel was. The Real Presence dwells among us. We live what Ezekiel was offered as a hope. God began the work of redeeming the world when He entered it on that dark night in Bethlehem and He healed our bodies when He clothed Himself in the flesh of the Virgin. Heaven begins now because God is with us and He remains with us.

Ezekiel's prophetic ministry bears witness to the fact that God does not abandon His people even in the darkest of times. When His people found themselves suffering in exile, God promised them His salvation through His prophet, just as He promises His salvation to each of one of us.

Ironically, during these weeks of preparing, the pace of this world feels hectic and its focus is on materialism. If ever there was a season in which we are tempted to be anxious and troubled about many things, December in the modern world is it. This time of year, the world can sometimes feel to be more a place of exile that at any other time. It's easy to become distracted. But there is one thing needful and He's tabernacled among us. He's waiting for us to adore Him under the veil of His Eucharistic Face. Perhaps the best way to prepare our hearts to receive Him is to visit Him dwelling among us, to stop and sit in recollected quiet at His feet. God will not take that from us, for in so doing we are choosing the better part.

KATHERINE JOHNSON

Come Holy Spirit, fill the hearts of your faithful
and kindle in them the fire of your love.
Send forth your Spirit and they shall be created.
And You shall renew the face of the earth.
O, God, who by the light of the Holy Spirit,
did instruct the hearts of the faithful,
grant that by the same Holy Spirit we may be truly wise
and ever enjoy His consolations, Through Christ Our Lord,
Amen.

LECTIO

What is the objective meaning of the text?

Who do I encounter here and what do they say?

What is the how, the where, the when & the why?

MEDITATIO

What does the biblical text say to me?

What personal message does the text have for me?

What effect does the text have on my life?

ORATIO

What do I say to the Lord in response to His word?

What does the Lord want for me? How do I ask for grace?

What is my song of of thanks for His gifts & praise for His glory?

CONTEMPLATIO

How does God see and judge reality? What conversion of mind, heart, and life is He asking of me today?

How has He conveyed His love for me in today's scripture?

Where is the beauty of His gifts and the goodness of His mercy?

How will I make my life a gift for others in charity?
What does God want me to do today?

TASKS & TO DOS

MEALS TO NOURISH

GIVING & PREPARING

KEEPING HOME

KINDNESS TO MYSELF

ACTIO

How did I progress in living the Word today?

Thursday, December 21
ROOTS & BRANCHES

Daniel

Daniel had heroic faith. He stands out as a sterling
example of a life firmly rooted in faith. That Daniel was a
man singularly focused on God was unequivocal. His life
was well-watered with fervent prayer and that prayer life
bore truly exceptional fruit. Everything Daniel did—from
eating to interpreting dreams—had God at the center.
Such a rich prayer life is sustained by a disciplined
prayer habit, a strong boldness, and, when necessary,
a counter-cultural defiance. No matter what, Daniel
returned again and again to his source of strength: God.
He lived his life ruled by prayer. When Daniel's devotion
to prayer was threatened, he knew that he would truly
die without it, and he had faith that God would save
him from whatever peril might threaten him if he only
persevered in prayer. We almost certainly don't face
the fiery furnaces of Daniel's friends or the menace of a
lion's den, but we will be tempted away from prayer and
towards the worship of false idols. Scripture gives us the
book of Daniel for times such as those.

DANIEL 6:10-13

Although Daniel knew that the document had been signed, he continued to go to his house, which had windows in its upper room open toward Jerusalem, and to get down on his knees three times a day to pray to his God and praise him, just as he had done previously. The conspirators came and found Daniel praying and seeking mercy before his God. Then they approached the king and said concerning the interdict, "O king! Did you not sign an interdict, that anyone who prays to anyone, divine or human, within thirty days except to you, O king, shall be thrown into a den of lions?" The king answered, "The thing stands fast, according to the law of the Medes and Persians, which cannot be revoked." Then they responded to the king, "Daniel, one of the exiles from Judah, pays no attention to you, O king, or to the interdict you have signed, but he is saying his prayers three times a day."

FOR FURTHER READING

ALL OF DANIEL 6

I don't have time. There are a million things on my to-do list, and even as I ponder that list, two more items have made themselves known. Cross out the scheduled routine doctor's appointment for one child, and replace it with an emergency dental appointment for another, thereby moving the routine appointment to another day already crowded with its own items. If I'm going to make the dentist on time, I need to quicken the pace of this morning.

It's obvious what is negotiable. Bump the prayer time to some vague "later" slot. No one is going to hold me accountable to that. No one else's health and welfare are contingent on my prayer time. Prayer gets bumped in favor of breakfast, finding someone's shoes, and getting to the dentist on time with a child who is appropriately groomed and has brushed her teeth. God will understand.

Of course He will. But maybe someone's health and welfare actually are dependent on my prayer time. And maybe Daniel is the hero of this cause. Daniel is at once incredibly brave and utterly dependent. His entire life is a testimony to unwavering faith. Daniel was fueled by prayer. What I know—because I've tried it both ways—is that my health and welfare are very much dependent on my prayer time. Without it, I fall apart, and we all suffer.

In this passage, Daniel is an esteemed member of king's court, about to be promoted to be the ruler of Persia. He must have thought of all the ways he was doing God's work. I wonder if he even said to himself that he could put off his prayers for thirty days because he was indispensable to the welfare of the people in his charge, and sacrificing prayer in order to survive to serve them just made prudent sense.

If that rationalization dawned on him, he dismissed it. Despite being threatened with his life, Daniel maintained his prayer routine. Unashamed and unafraid, he prayed with his faith on his sleeve for all to see. He was diligent and forthright, and he made sure that everyone understood who was Lord of his life. Daniel's life was built on prayer, and he was blessed with a clear and unwavering understanding that without God, he was nothing, and his life was not worth living.

Prayer was such a habit in Daniel's life that when the time came to be tested in his faithfulness to it, his path was clear. He already prayed three times a day in a very specific way, so the mere keeping of this habit would also be a perfect public witness to his faith in the true God. He wasn't performing for the sake of making his point; he was acting in faith just as he did on every ordinary day. In his discipline, Daniel finds the freedom to be authentic. This is the same prayer habit that yielded Daniel the extraordinary prophet. It is the same prayer habit that will sustain him in the lion's den. For Daniel, prayer is more precious than life itself. Regular, intentional prayer is the discipline that is the most important to the health and welfare of Daniel.

And of me.

And probably of you, too.

Daniel knew that if he prayed, he'd end up in a lion's den. And still he prayed. To him, being cut off from his life source—the God who animated him—was worse than not living at all. He was radically committed to a life of dialogue with his Lord. The entire book of Daniel is one precious, beautiful testimony of faith after another. God always shows up for Daniel.

And Daniel always, always shows up for God.

Do you?

ELIZABETH FOSS

Come Holy Spirit, fill the hearts of your faithful
and kindle in them the fire of your love.
Send forth your Spirit and they shall be created.
And You shall renew the face of the earth.
O, God, who by the light of the Holy Spirit,
did instruct the hearts of the faithful,
grant that by the same Holy Spirit we may be truly wise
and ever enjoy His consolations, Through Christ Our Lord,
Amen.

LECTIO

What is the objective meaning of the text?

Who do I encounter here and what do they say?

What is the how, the where, the when & the why?

MEDITATIO

What does the biblical text say to me?

What personal message does the text have for me?

What effect does the text have on my life?

ORATIO

What do I say to the Lord in response to His word?

What does the Lord want for me? How do I ask for grace? What is my song of of thanks for His gifts & praise for His glory?

CONTEMPLATIO

How does God see and judge reality? What conversion of mind, heart, and life is He asking of me today?

How has He conveyed His love for me in today's scripture?

Where is the beauty of His gifts and the goodness of His mercy?

How will I make my life a gift for others in charity?
What does God want me to do today?

TASKS & TO DOS

MEALS TO NOURISH

GIVING & PREPARING

KEEPING HOME

KINDNESS TO MYSELF

ACTIO

How did I progress in living the Word today?

Friday, December 22
ROOTS & BRANCHES

Joseph

Saint Joseph's life did not follow along a predictable
path. He was astonished by the pregnancy of his
betrothed, married her, and lead a very pregnant Mary
on a grueling journey to Bethlehem that culminated with
a birth in a barn. Then, there were nearly immediate
threats on his baby's life, two desert crossings with a
nursing baby, life in a foreign land, and utter dependence
on God for the next set of instructions and provision
once he got there. All of the inconveniences and detours
were planned by God in fulfillment of the Scriptures.
We can be certain that they didn't make much sense
to Joseph at the time. But his life was very much about
Jesus, and not at all about himself. He was the good and
faithful shepherd—the wise protector of the Holy family
whose protection was ultimately God's providence.

MATTHEW 1:18-25

Now the birth of Jesus the Messiah took place in this way. When his mother Mary had been engaged to Joseph, but before they lived together, she was found to be with child from the Holy Spirit. Her husband Joseph, being a righteous man and unwilling to expose her to public disgrace, planned to dismiss her quietly. But just when he had resolved to do this, an angel of the Lord appeared to him in a dream and said, "Joseph, son of David, do not be afraid to take Mary as your wife, for the child conceived in her is from the Holy Spirit. She will bear a son, and you are to name him Jesus, for he will save his people from their sins." All this took place to fulfill what had been spoken by the Lord through the prophet: "Look, the virgin shall conceive and bear a son,

and they shall name him Emmanuel,"

which means, "God is with us." When Joseph awoke from sleep, he did as the angel of the Lord commanded him; he took her as his wife, but had no marital relations with her until she had borne a son; and he named him Jesus.

FOR FURTHER READING

MATTHEW 2

MATTHEW 13: 55

MATTHEW 1: 1-16

LUKE 3: 23-38

My father married my mother after knowing her for only four months. When asked why they moved so quickly Dad always said, "The first time I saw your mom, she was receiving Communion. I knew she was the one."

My dad also wanted a large family, and my mother loved him enough to agree to eight children in ten years. Whenever my mother worried about providing for us, Dad reminded her of all God had done for them. "God is faithful," my father used to say. "He will not allow us to languish."

Despite struggling with his own issues, my Dad trusted in God's timing for his relationship with my mother and provision for his family. This trust is a virtue I always wanted, but often felt I lacked. Even during the hardest days with my disabled daughter Courtney, after God provided miracle after miracle, I'm ashamed to admit I still struggled to trust Him.

But trust isn't a static thing. For it to grow deep roots, it must be tested. When I was in middle school, my father was laid off. For three months, he applied for job after job. Despite all the rejections, he relied on prayer and daily Mass to sustain him during his search. Our family prayed the rosary every night for Dad to find a job. Despite the financial strain, my parents showed us what faith looked like. I never saw tears or distress, just fidelity to God.

When the last severance check arrived, my father was still unemployed. That morning, he attended Mass while my mother went to the grocery store. Since she didn't know when she'd be able to make another trip, she was discouraged and confused. She prayed through every aisle. She laid her family's need at the foot of the Cross, yet was still waiting. My father had sent out over 100 resumes. What else did God want?

When my mother arrived home, she found my father inside speaking on the phone. When he hung up, he had a big smile on his face. "God did it. He got me a job!" It wasn't a perfect solution. Dad had to work out of state for an entire year, but my parents just praised God for His provision.

Even Saint Joseph grappled with discerning the right thing. He loved Mary and wanted to protect her, but he was confused. When the angel appeared in His dream, Joseph never questioned the instructions; he just did as God asked. Once Joseph knew God had spoken to him, he moved swiftly, despite not having a clue as to how it would all turn out.

I'm also amazed at Mary's trust in Joseph. She told him the truth and trusted that he would do the right thing. Like my parents, Mary and Joseph agreed to the plan God set forth, not knowing how the story would end. They loved God and one another enough to just keep moving, allowing Him to work through all the details.

This level of trust has always been just beyond my reach. I've always struggled with fully relying upon God's faithfulness. In return, He always brings me to the edge before proving that He's not only listening, but also providing for me. It's a game He and I play; I cry and whine about a problem, and God waits until I'm blubbered out long enough to listen and pray and believe Him. That's when He steps in and reminds me that, like Joseph and Mary, He holds me close to His heart. He hears my cries. And He will never forsake me.

As Catholic Christians, we face this struggle daily. Do we trust God with our problems without knowing how it's all going to work out? Can we walk by faith and not by sight? During this Advent season, let us ask Saint Joseph and Our Blessed Mother to intercede for us to trust God in the journey, regardless how difficult, regardless where it leads.

MARY LENABURG

Come Holy Spirit, fill the hearts of your faithful
and kindle in them the fire of your love.
Send forth your Spirit and they shall be created.
And You shall renew the face of the earth.
O, God, who by the light of the Holy Spirit,
did instruct the hearts of the faithful,
grant that by the same Holy Spirit we may be truly wise
and ever enjoy His consolations, Through Christ Our Lord,
Amen.

LECTIO

What is the objective meaning of the text?

Who do I encounter here and what do they say?

What is the how, the where, the when & the why?

MEDITATIO

What does the biblical text say to me?

What personal message does the text have for me?

What effect does the text have on my life?

ORATIO

What do I say to the Lord in response to His word?

What does the Lord want for me? How do I ask for grace? What is my song of of thanks for His gifts & praise for His glory?

CONTEMPLATIO

How does God see and judge reality? What conversion of mind, heart, and life is He asking of me today?

How has He conveyed His love for me in today's scripture?

Where is the beauty of His gifts and the goodness of His mercy?

How will I make my life a gift for others in charity?
What does God want me to do today?

TASKS & TO DOS

MEALS TO NOURISH

GIVING & PREPARING

ACTIO

KEEPING HOME

KINDNESS TO MYSELF

How did I progress in living the Word today?

Saturday, December 23
SCRIPTURE MEMORY

This week, as we celebrate Christmas, and bask in its afterglow, we present ourselves again to the Lord as His handmaidens--- ready, willing, and glad to serve.

Memorizing Scripture makes it our own. When we commit it to our hearts, we always have it to carry wherever we go. This week, remember that the Lord will strengthen you to the end. It's a journey, and He's taking it with you.

Today is a day to rest and be grateful (as much as you can two days before Christmas!). Take some time to look over your journaling from the week, to read a little more, to catch up on days when you didn't have as much time as you would have liked.

Spend a few moments looking carefully at our memory verses, to burn the image into your brain. Then write them yourself on the weekly planning page and read them again and again when you refer to the tasks of the your weekly to-dos.

One more thing: if there is a child in your life, teach these words to him or her. They will serve that child for a lifetime. Don't be surprised when the child memorizes more easily than you do, even when the verses are longer. This memory work is a gift, a legacy. Hiding the Word of God in the heart of child is stocking his soul with saving grace. Together, take on this joyful endeavor. We're right there with you.

Luke 1:38

Here am I, the servant of the Lord; let it be with me according to your word.

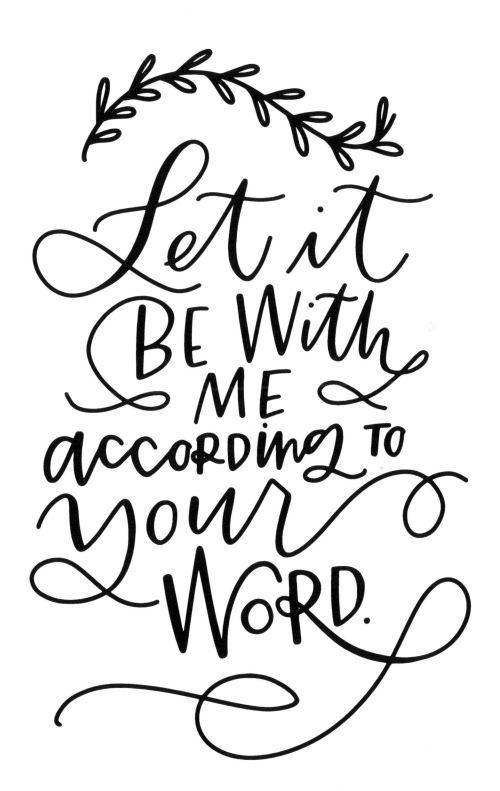

LUKE 1:38

Fourth Week of Advent

Week of Sunday, December 24

SUNDAY | DECEMBER 24

MONDAY | DECEMBER 25

TUESDAY | DECEMBER 26

WEDNESDAY | DECEMBER 27

THURSDAY | DECEMBER 28

FRIDAY | DECEMBER 29

SATURDAY | DECEMBER 30

feast day celebration ideas

Fourth Week of Advent

memory verse

give + prepare

LUKE 1:38

prayer requests

Sunday, December 24
FOURTH SUNDAY OF ADVENT

LUKE 1:26-38

In the sixth month the angel Gabriel was sent by God to a town in Galilee called Nazareth, to a virgin engaged to a man whose name was Joseph, of the house of David. The virgin's name was Mary. And he came to her and said, "Greetings, favored one! The Lord is with you." But she was much perplexed by his words and pondered what sort of greeting this might be. The angel said to her, "Do not be afraid, Mary, for you have found favor with God. And now, you will conceive in your womb and bear a son, and you will name him Jesus. He will be great, and will be called the Son of the Most High, and the Lord God will give to him the throne of his ancestor David. He will reign over the house of Jacob forever, and of his kingdom there will be no end." Mary said to the angel, "How can this be, since I am a virgin?" The angel said to her, "The Holy Spirit will come upon you, and the power of the Most High will overshadow you; therefore the child to be born will be holy; he will be called Son of God. And now, your relative Elizabeth in her old age has also conceived a son; and this is the sixth month for her who was said to be barren. For nothing will be impossible with God." Then Mary said, "Here am I, the servant of the Lord; let it be with me according to your word." Then the angel departed from her.

FOR FURTHER READING

ROMANS 16:25-27

2 SAMUEL 7:1-5, 8B-12, 14A, 16

We arrive here on this Sunday with a liturgical urgency. Hurry! Read and ponder the Annunciation because tonight it will be Christmas.

Shortest pregnancy ever.

We sit with Mary in a room that is suddenly filled with the light of an angel. Gabriel tells the startled teenager that she is full of grace and has found favor with God. She doesn't deserve the honor that God will bestow with her assent. He makes Himself make a gift to her. Mary is the personification of perfect humility. She knows that she has not earned His favor.

Despite the assurance that God is fully with her, she is troubled by the angel's words. A million thoughts collide in her mind: the impossibility of it all (naturally speaking); the trouble that is to come when she is found to be pregnant; the honest, human fear that pregnancy strikes in almost every woman's heart. So many unknowns, so many opportunities to relinquish to the Lord those things over which mere humans have no control! Mary faces all of this in a split second with perfect humility. Because of grace, she understands that God is in control and that all things will work together for the good according to His plan (Romans 8:28). She knows that it is God who has favored her and it is God who will equip her. Pride never stands between the Virgin and her "yes."

Grace is not always a gentle breeze. Grace can be quite severe. For Mary, with this grace came certain and intense suffering. She embraced an unfathomably severe grace. She paused and pondered and allowed for the possibility that the pain was the path to His mercy. When Gabriel spoke to Mary, he spoke into our doubts. He told her to be assured that this really was the grace of God and to let that sure knowledge seep into her soul and take away her human fear.

Grace doesn't transport us from suffering; indeed, it transported Mary directly into suffering, nearly immediately. Grace is not the intercession of a benevolent God who sweeps the heroine away from suffering. Grace isn't the gentle breath that blows us past the pain to the promised happiness.

Instead, there is grace in the struggle itself. Grace changes us, and change hurts. Marked by the stain of sin, handicapped by the imperfections of a fallen world, it is our nature to fight suffering instead of leaning into it. Our "yes" often sounds less like "Let it be done to me according to your word" than it does, "Okay, God, but please don't let it hurt." It hurts. Grace is not the anesthesia; it's the incision.

Can you welcome the surgical strike and embrace the pain, knowing with the confidence of Mary that God will use the difficult circumstances to change you, to make you more like Him?

You belong to the Lord. Grace will find you. Can you recognize it in the hard moments, the ones that don't twinkle like lights on a Christmas tree, but instead reek of the dung in a stable at midnight in the piercing cold? Can you see that God came in glory for the dirty, smelly, darkest moments of your life. Can you know grace in the pain?

We are hours from the jubilation of the Solemnity. We are hours from the church come to life with the voices singing Gloria in excelcis Deo. We are hours from the merrymaking and the gifts and the tables heaped with food. We are also a few short moments from short tempers and hurt feelings and tricky family dynamics. We are within a hair's breadth of disappointments and loneliness and the emptiness of a holiday that doesn't live up to the hype.

It's holy day. A holy day. A sacred, consecrated, hallowed day. Christmas is a day full of grace. Can you recognize the grace Christmas holds for you this year?

ELIZABETH FOSS

Come Holy Spirit, fill the hearts of your faithful
and kindle in them the fire of your love.
Send forth your Spirit and they shall be created.
And You shall renew the face of the earth.
O, God, who by the light of the Holy Spirit,
did instruct the hearts of the faithful,
grant that by the same Holy Spirit we may be truly wise
and ever enjoy His consolations, Through Christ Our Lord,
Amen.

LECTIO

What is the objective meaning of the text?

Who do I encounter here and what do they say?

What is the how, the where, the when & the why?

MEDITATIO

What does the biblical text say to me?

What personal message does the text have for me?

What effect does the text have on my life?

ORATIO

What do I say to the Lord in response to His word?

What does the Lord want for me? How do I ask for grace? What is my song of of thanks for His gifts & praise for His glory?

CONTEMPLATIO

How does God see and judge reality? What conversion of mind, heart, and life is He asking of me today?

How has He conveyed His love for me in today's scripture?

Where is the beauty of His gifts and the goodness of His mercy?

How will I make my life a gift for others in charity?
What does God want me to do today?

TASKS & TO DOS

MEALS TO NOURISH

GIVING & PREPARING

KEEPING HOME

KINDNESS TO MYSELF

ACTIO

How did I progress in living the Word today?

Monday, December 25
CHRISTMAS DAY

LUKE 2:15-20

When the angels had left them and gone into heaven, the shepherds said to one another, "Let us go now to Bethlehem and see this thing that has taken place, which the Lord has made known to us." So they went with haste and found Mary and Joseph, and the child lying in the manger. When they saw this, they made known what had been told them about this child; and all who heard it were amazed at what the shepherds told them. But Mary treasured all these words and pondered them in her heart. The shepherds returned, glorifying and praising God for all they had heard and seen, as it had been told them.

FOR FURTHER READING

ISAIAH 62:11-12

TITUS 3:4-7

In those "rest and be grateful moments," after a healthy birth of a healthy baby, there is a peace that comes with quiet joy. The worry and the work are past. Contentment settles, a thick sigh of relief blanketed over extraordinary happiness. These are the moments when praying mothers know to the core of our beings that God is near.

I cannot even imagine what that peace must feel like when the baby Himself is God.

In the hushed stable, punctuated by animal grunting and the noises of the night, Mary accepted her visitors and heard their praises. No doubt, she smiled the weary smile of a mother who has labored well and then learned what unfathomable love it is to hold her newborn. She saw how all the pieces had fallen into place in most extraordinary ways, and she knew that God's provision was nothing less than a carefully planned miracle.

As she pondered, Mary was grateful. One by one, looking around that dank stable, she took note of what was happening and what she was hearing. She made her gratitude list, tucking each item away in her heart.

Christmas is a time for being very grateful. What are the things you want to remember today? For what things are you so grateful that you want to be sure to ponder them in your heart? Pen your gratitude in the coming week on the following pages.

ELIZABETH FOSS

171

A NOTE FROM
THE ARTIST

*When I heard that the title of this Advent journal was Rooted In Hope, I
thought of organic shapes, plants, and of course, roots. I tried to think about
a steadfast plant whose roots take strong hold into the earth, can weather
environmental extremes and still produce fruit. I also thought about the
word 'hope'. Initially what sprung to mind was Noah's dove, bringing an
olive branch to the Ark and the hope that dry land was finally near. But a
dove with an olive branch has historically been used to represent peace. Still,
the olive branch -more specifically- the olive tree kept coming back to mind.
After reading about the nature of the olive tree; how during the life of Jesus,
olive oil was used for both religious and medicinal purposes, for lighting
lamps, the olive fruit for nourishing the body; and remembering that we
use olive oil today in as a sacramental Holy oil and Chrism: particularly
to symbolize strength in our vocation as Christians; and after reading
the multitude of biblical references regarding the sturdiness and ability
of the olive tree to withstand harsh weather, living on for thousands (yes,
thousands!) of years, comparing the tree's steadfastness to the covenant God
makes with his chosen people, the Jews, I knew that it had to be the plant
which should symbolize how we root ourselves in the hope of Christ's birth
this Advent. Life goes through similar extremes: when everything seems
to be falling apart, our hope, so deeply rooted in God's grace, and Christ's
redemption is the only thing that will keep us going. Throughout the
journal, I've included the dove, who as a God's creation, did indeed bring
Noah that hope— the hope of a new beginning, and yes, the hope of peace in
a final resting place. For us today, that hope is rooted in the infant Jesus. I
hope this translates in my work, and that you take joy in it.*

CAROLYN SVELLINGER

We knew that the Advent book would sparkle brightly with Carolyn's
special touch. As we continue to design and publish scripture studies
we look for artists like Carolyn, who not only take the time and energy
to create quality designs but also take care of those around her. We are
grateful for her creative collaboration and look forward to Carolyn's
art career and art shop, Brass & Mint Co.

THE WRITERS

CARLY BUCKHOLZ studied poetry at the University of Virginia before earning a Master's in Higher Education. After five years in Charlottesville, she has moved across the Atlantic for a teaching fellowship in southern England. There, she will teach literature and work in student affairs for the next year. Often next to a pile of books, Carly spends most of her time trying to convince her friends to read more poetry and baking scones. She enjoys writing about her family, her faith, and the Blue Ridge Mountains.

MICAELA DARR lives in Southern California and is a happy wife to her husband, and mother to 6 charming kiddos (with another bun in the oven). In her former life, she was an elementary and middle school teacher outside the home. Now, as a homeschooling mom, she does both those jobs (and many more) for far less money, but also more joy. She renewed her love of writing by starting a blog when her family took a 2 year adventure to South Korea, and has since contributed her writing to several other Catholic websites, and 2 books set to be published in 2018. Her latest out-of-the-home adventure is planning a small Catholic women's conference that aims to strengthen women on their journey to be closer to the God who loves them.

ELIZABETH FOSS is a wife, mother, and grandmother. She's happy curled up with a good book or tinkering with a turn of phrase. Long walks make her heart sing and occasionally cause her to break into a run. Though she travels frequently, it's usually only between northern Virginia and her beloved Charlottesville, or to the weekend's dictated soccer or dance destination.

 KATY GREINER is a daughter, a sister, a recent graduate, and a high school teacher who's newly facing the real world. In that project, she's fueled by music, books, a strong cup of tea, good conversation, and hearing God laugh.

ANA HAHN is a wife of nine years and mother of five. She enjoys educating her three school-aged daughters at home and playing planes with her two toddler boys. In her rare spare time she works on making her home bright and cheerful and sharing bits of that, as well as other motherhood musings on her blog, Time Flies When You're Having Babies.

KATHERINE JOHNSON is a wife of 22 years and the mother of seven children, spanning kindergarten to college. She's made finding God among the pots and the posies her life's work, because most often He makes Himself known in the profoundly ordinary moments of her everyday life. An enthusiastic knitter, an adventurous home cook, and a voracious reader, Katherine has a heart for all things domestic. She keeps a home, tends a garden, and educates her children in Dallas, Texas.

MARY LENABURG is a writer, speaker, wife and mother sharing her witness and testimony about God's Redeeming love. Mary has served her local parish in many roles, including Liturgy Coordinator, Youth Ministry, and Confirmation Preparation Instructor. Now she travels the country and speaks to groups of all ages about God's Redeeming love and that faith is the courage to want what God wants for us, even if we cannot see where the path leads. Mary lives in Northern Virginia with her husband of 29 years and her grown son. She continues to embrace her father's advice: "Never quit, never give up, never lose your faith. It's the one reason you walk this earth. For God chose this time and place just for you, so make the most of it."

ALLISON MCGINLEY lives with her husband and two kids in northern Virginia. When she's not dancing with her daughter or learning about Legos from her son, she writes, sings with a local worship band, and takes pictures of beautiful things. She shares her inspirational photography prints in her Etsy shop, "Be Not Afraid Prints."

COLLEEN MITCHELL is a wife, bringer upper of boys, Gospel adventurer, wanna-be saint, author and speaker. She is the author of the award-winning *Who Does He Say You Are: Women Transformed by Christ in the Gospels*, and the soon to be released *When We Were Eve:*

THE WRITERS

Uncovering the Woman God Created You to Be. Her latest adventure has taken her from the jungle of Costa Rica where she and her family have served as missionaries for the last six years, to the wilds of a sixth grade classroom in Fort Wayne, Indiana, where she is still living her mission to give everyone she meets just a little Jesus.

HEATHER RENSHAW is a wife and mother of five living in the missionary territory of the Pacific Northwest. She rarely turns down an opportunity for deep conversation, loud singing, good eating, or silent Adoration. Heather is the author of an eight-week study on the Beatitudes and a contributing author of *All Things Girl: Truth For Teens*. She is currently writing her first book for Catholic Moms. When she's not tackling the myriad tasks of her domestic church, Heather enjoys speaking at events and connecting via Twitter and Instagram (@ RealCatholicMom). Heather may be found at www.RealCatholicMom. com.

KATHRYN WHITAKER, a native Texan, is a wife and mom to six kids, teen to toddler. She shares her perspective on marriage, motherhood, college football, Texas BBQ, and her Catholic faith with honesty and authenticity on her blog www.teamwhitaker.org. She's a frequent guest on Sirius XM's "The Jennifer Fulwiler Show" but all her kids really care about is what time dinner's ready. In her spare time, she operates her own graphic design business, working primarily with Catholic campus ministry programs around the country.

KATE WICKER is a Catholic wife, mom of five, recovering perfectionist, speaker, and the author of *Getting Past Perfect: How to Find Joy & Grace in the Messiness of Motherhood* and *Weightless: Making Peace with Your Body*. Kate is a senior writer for Catholic Digest and a monthly guest on Relevant Radio's Morning Air Show and Spirit in the Morning. She has written for numerous regional and national media, and she has appeared on television and radio outlets. She also has an "almost finished" novel in the works that's been "almost finished" since her she was pregnant with her third baby nearly a decade ago. To learn more about her work and life, visit KateWicker.com.

THE ARTISTS

CAROLYN SVELLINGER is an artist/illustrator living in Cincinnati. She and her husband have 5 children— all boys! Carolyn is blessed with the ability to homeschool her children and run her own business selling prints of her artwork from her Etsy shop: Brass & Mint Co. She also enjoys knitting and photography. Instagram is her hangout.

KRISTIN FOSS is the Art Director for Take Up & Read. Kristin is a self-taught watercolor artist who focuses on bright, detailed florals. With a paint brush in her hand and fresh blooms in a vase, she finds peace in God's Word while putting brush to paper. She enjoys creative cooking, thrift stores, and nature walks. You can find her at joyfulmornings.com

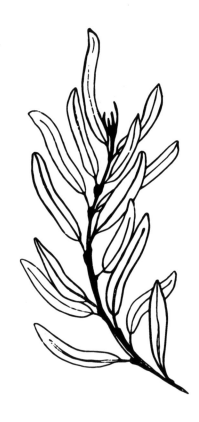

take up & READ

Take Up & Read is committed to creating printed journals
that you can hold in your hands and touch with your pens.
We collected our conversations with God. These volumes
allow us to both commit at least a little time daily to honest
conversation with God in His Word, and to dig more deeply
and respond more carefully
when we have the grace to do so.

We know that the Bible is God's story for us. And we want to
live in the center of that holy narrative every day. We want
God's Word to give us words for one another,
a common language of love in Him.

God's Word endures—across the seasons of a woman's life
it is the constant. He is faithful every day. In every restless
night, in every joyous celebration, in all the ordinary days in
between, we can and do seek the voice
of our Lord in His Holy Scripture.

We take our name from the pages of Saint Augustine's
Confessions. Now a Doctor of the Church, Augustine was
living a life of miserable debauchery when he was compelled
by the Holy Spirit to take up his Bible and read it. His entire
world changed in a moment
of conversation with Word.

We believe that ours can, too—on an ordinary day, in an
ordinary living room or coffee shop or college dorm, to
ordinary women. We pray it is so every single day.

BIBLIOGRAPHY

Hahn, Scott. Catholic Bible dictionary. Doubleday, 2009.

Sheridan, Mark. Genesis 12-50 (Ancient Christian Commentary on Scripture: Old Testament, Volume II). IVP Academic, 2002.

Unger, Merrill, and R.K. Harrison. The New Unger's Bible Dictionary. Moody Publishers, 2006.

"VERBUM DOMINI." Verbum Domini: Post-Synodal Apostolic Exhortation on the Word of God in the Life and Mission of the Church (30 September 2010) | BENEDICT XVI, w2.vatican.va/content/benedict-xvi/en/apost_exhortations/documents/hf_ben-xvi_exh_20100930_verbum-domini.html.

Yee, Gale A., et al. The historical writings. Fortress Press, 2016.

COLOPHON

This book was printed by CreateSpace, on 55# paper with an interior black and white.
Typefaces used include Freight Text Pro, Futura PT and Montserrat.
The cover is printed in full color with a soft touch matte, full laminate.
Finished size 7"x10".

Printed in Great Britain
by Amazon